Communicating is fundamental to eve

fail to assess whether we are maximizing our effectiveness. Did we communicate clearly? How did our communications influence the understanding of others? Did we achieve the desired result? The how to's and tips found in each chapter of this book are worth adopting.

—**Peter Rietkerk**, General Manager, South San Joaquin Irrigation District

Communication and miscommunications happen throughout the day and can lead to misunderstanding, hurt feelings and, sadly, violence. This book is chock-full of examples of how to make sure your communication is intentional, positive, and designed to be embraced by the recipient.

—**Marshall Goldsmith**, #1 New York Times bestselling author of *Triggers, MOJO,* and *What Got You Here Won't Get You There*

Talk about a book written for busy leaders! *Consequential Communication in Turbulent Times* is action-oriented with Diana's tried-and-true tips outlined in the back for easy reference. If you need a case study or specifics on how to apply the tip, then go to the relevant chapter and get what you need to ensure that your communication is authentic, heard, and understood.

Susan Fowler, bestselling author, *Master Your Motivation: Three Scientific Truths for Achieving Your Goals*

.

CONSEQUENTIAL COMMUNICATION IN TURBULENT TIMES

A Practical Guide to Leadership

by

Diana Peterson-More

ISBN: 978-1-7336146-0-3 (paperback)
ISBN: 978-1-7336146-1-0 (e-book)

Interior and cover design: Rachel Royer
Typesetting: Lori Weidert

Printed in the United States of America

To those I love most, and who have enriched my life beyond measure: son, Nathanial; daughters, Kelsey and Juliana; grandson, Matthias; and granddaughters, Reese and Remy; with love from Moms, Nonna Diana, Mimi

CONTENTS

Preface..ix

Acknowledgments...xi

About the Author xiii

1 What is Communication?.. 1

2 Make It Easy for Them to Say Yes................................... 9

3 The Platinum Rule of Communication....................... 23

4 Strategic Communication 31

5 Listening, Asking, and Telling.......................................39

6 "I" Statements and "Acts and Facts"........................... 51

7 Check for Understanding 57

8 The Two-For-One Rule, Timing is Everything,
and the Power of Positive Feedback........................... 63

9 Perception is Reality 71

10 The Sting of Emotional Communication...................77

11 Workplace Communication in the
Era of Technology...81

12 The Powers of Apology and Humility
in the Workplace 89

13 That's a Wrap...95

PREFACE

"What we've got here is a failure to communicate," said Captain to Luke in the 1967 movie *Cool Hand Luke.* In this era of "alternate facts," "fake news," and "if you say it loud enough and often enough, it's the truth," clear, concise, and consequential communication is imperative. Communication is at the heart of all human relationships; it is the glue that binds us. Miscommunications, on the other hand, can lead to misunderstanding, mistrust, suspicion, anger, and even violence. How do we avoid that? How do we maintain the civility that is a force factor in public and private life?

The late-great Gerald Rosen, a contracts professor at Loyola Law School used to say, "If you can't get them on the merry-go-round, get them on the swings; if you can't get them on the swings, get them on the slide; if you can't get them on the slide, get them on the monkey bars." Having heard those words lo these many years ago, I haven't a clue as to what contracts matter he was referring, but those evocative childhood images of a day at the park persisted and remain with me.

I've come to realize that his admonition had little to do with traditional contracts (as in the quid pro quo/this-for-that barter world in which we live) and everything to do with communication. Some of us take in information by listening. Some of us take in information by engaging in the dialogue. Some of us take in information by reading. Some of us hear first, and then need follow-up in writing.

There are multiple ways in which to give and receive information. There is no right way or wrong way, there are merely many ways. The trick is to ferret out the best way to communicate with the person the communicator is trying to communicate with!

This is especially true in the turbulent times in which we live, punctuated by false information and fear of other. At the same time we are maneuvering through an increasingly smaller world peopled by a multiplicity of cultures, languages, differing norms, and notions of what is "right" and what is "wrong."

Consequential Communication in Turbulent Times is filled with stories that have been gathered from over 30 years in the field, working with tens of thousands of individuals worldwide. As Joe Friday would say in that long-ago television show, *Dragnet,* "The names have been changed to protect the innocent." However, their stories are here, and rich with lessons to learn about communication and miscommunication.

Are you looking for a communications "ah-ha" moment? If so, take the journey through this book, and you might pick up a trick or two to add to your bag-of-tricks.

Diana Peterson-More

ACKNOWLEDGMENTS

Through the stories in this book, there are many who have contributed, and for whom the book was written. All of them should be acknowledged. Whether they figure out who they are will be a mystery.

One person alone stands out as the individual who encouraged me in too many ways to enumerate, and for whom I gratefully acknowledge: Julie Winkle Giulioni, the international best-selling co-author of *Help Them Grow or Watch Them Go: Career Conversations Organizations Need and Employees Want.*

Julie, you are the best!

ABOUT THE AUTHOR

 Diana Peterson-More, an employment lawyer, manager, officer, and corporate human resources executive, left a Fortune 200 company to launch The Organizational Effectiveness Group, LLC. Through strategic planning, team work, training, and coaching, Peterson-More's company focuses on services and products that align individuals with organizational goals. She is a community volunteer, active hiker, international traveler, and a proud parent: "Of all the things I've been or done or yet hope to be or do, being the mother of three amazing children is by far my biggest accomplishment."

WHAT IS COMMUNICATION?

There are doubtless as many definitions of communication as there are ways in which we communicate. Consider all of the following: how we dress and wear our hair; how we walk, sit, and stand; how we present ourselves—whether we make eye contact, smile, or meet another's gaze. Think about how we speak, project, write, and use social media, and how we take in information and respond. These are some of the many ways that we project ourselves, consciously or unconsciously, that communicate who we are in the world and in the workplace.

This practical guide to communication in the workplace is focused on one simple concept: At the heart of workplace communication, the communicator—typically the boss—is trying to induce another person—often the employee—to perform a given task. I believe that workplace communication often relies on the art of persuading another individual to do what you want her or him to do, and that it is in their best interest to do it.

If communication in the workplace involves persuading others to do what you want them to do, what are some practical tips to do so?

The How To's

1. Communicate the instructions in a manner that the employee can understand.

2. Share the goal to be achieved and your employee's important role in achieving it.

3. Thank the employee for a job well done.

4. Offer to help, or to explain why you are not available to do so.

1. **Communicate the instructions in a manner that the employee can understand.** This sounds simple enough, and undoubtedly something we all think we do. However, "the proof is in the pudding." Did you get what you wanted? Was the task completed to your satisfaction? Was it on time? If you can answer yes to these, then you hit the mark.

    If not, how did you communicate—verbally, in writing, or both? Did you check for understanding from the other party? Did you ask the person to repeat the request in his own words, or ask him to send you an e-mail detailing what he believes you want, and how he plans to deliver?

    Try one or more of these methods next time.

2. **Share the goal to be achieved and your employee's important role in achieving it.** We know what we mean, what we want, and how it fits into the big picture. Sharing that big-picture information allows people to see how important their contributions are.

    Consider this: Ruby Receptionist worked for a nonprofit that aids the homeless. One day Bob Boss told her to stay late and send out 200 letters. Bob knew that Ruby was a single mother, that her son was in a childcare center, and that she would have to pay a late fee. In addition, Ruby's son would be the last child at the center, and she worried that he would feel abandoned.

    Nonetheless, Ruby stayed late and paid overtime at the childcare center. The next day, Bob came into the office, walked right by Ruby, and said nothing.

    She said, "I will never stay late again."

    What if? Bob had come to Ruby and said, "I have an extremely important assignment for you. We are $10,000 short of our fundraising goal, which means we will not be able to help all of our homeless clients. I hope that through this appeal letter, we can raise the money."

Can you stay late to send it out? I know your son needs to be picked up. How will this affect you? How can I help?"

What if? The next day, Bob said "Thank you, Ruby, for staying last night. I hope that the overtime pay you receive in your next check will cover any late fees from the childcare center. If not, let me know and I'll see what I can do to help out."

Had Bob done that, Ruby would have felt good about her contribution, and appreciated by her boss. She might even have become an eager-to-please employee that takes the initiative to achieve the nonprofit's goals.

---

3. **Thank the employee for a job well done.** This is such a simple thing to do, yet it is something we often fail at in the workplace.

A common piece of feedback employees give about their bosses' communication style is "I always know when I screw up, but I never know when I do well." A practical piece of advice: Don't be phony or fake, but surely in the course of each week there is an employee that you can thank for having done something special, and an attaboy or an attagirl you can give for a job well done.

Consider this: Employees working for Simon Supervisor, SVP of Finance for a major entertainment firm offered this comment about his ability to give feedback: "I only know when I screw up and never know when I do well." After incorporating the above advice into his leadership toolkit, he witnessed a complete turnaround in his ability to get others to do what he wanted, and what the company needed.

Within six months, employees from other departments were clamoring to work for him. Why? Because they, too, wanted to be appreciated and thanked for their contributions to the company's goals.

4. **Offer to help, or to explain why you are not available to do so.** If possible, the boss herself should stay late, roll up her sleeves, and help. If not, she should explain why she can't stay, and ask someone else to pitch in.

Case Study 1.1

While handing him a 25-page document at 5:15 p.m. as she walked out the door, Cecilia CEO told Edward Executive Assistant to "take this document, copy it, and send it to Board members Bryan, Bethany, and Bob—but not to Karl or Karen—before you leave. Understand?" Thinking he got it, Edward nodded.

Edward was a single parent who needed to leave by 5:30 sharp to pick up his children from daycare. He had been a stay-at-home father before his divorce, so he needed this new job to get his foot back into the workplace door. Cecilia knew this when she hired him two months earlier. She had indicated during the interview process that this was a "family-friendly workplace," and that she would accommodate his parental needs.

Edward hurriedly copied the document, noting that some of the pages were slightly askew, and leaving the original in the copier. He placed the documents into envelopes, made mailing labels for Bryan, Bethany, and Karl, and walked down to the mailroom in the basement before leaving the building.

The next day, Molly Manager, the office gossip, found the forgotten document in the copier. She couldn't resist reading it before returning the document to Edward. Molly learned that Cecilia CEO was calling a special board meeting for 4:00 p.m. that day to vote to remove Karl and Karen from the Board. The document detailed that a private investigator had discovered that the two board members were divulging corporate secrets to a competitor.

At 4:00, CEO Cecelia went into the boardroom to find that no one was there. She was furious, and called Edward into her office and yelled "what happened, you idiot? Where are the board members?" Suffice it to say, when the dust settled both Cecilia CEO and Edward Executive Assistant were fired.

What Went Wrong?

Cecelia's Point of View

Cecelia stated "I assumed that since Edward nodded, he understood my very clear instructions."

"Edward should have known that anything going to board members should be sent overnight, delivery next morning, with receipt requested."

"Since Edward is a professional, he should have known that he needed to stay late to ensure the job was done correctly, and that, of course, overtime would be approved. Surely he had made plans to have his children picked up when he needed to work late."

Edward's Point of View

Cecelia's directions were unclear. How would I know that it needed to go out overnight, with return receipt requested? I'm new here."

"I only had 15 minutes before I had to leave to get my children, and Cecilia knew this when I was hired. In addition, there is a strict rule against overtime and Cecilia didn't say I should stay late. Even if she had, what was I going to do about my children?"

Consider this: How could this have turned out if Cecilia had given Edward different directions and partnered with him on the activity?

"Edward, I have an extremely important assignment that I am going to entrust to you. It involves the Board of Directors. Unfortunately,

I can't stay because I must meet with an outside consultant whose work impacts directly on the issue I need your help with. I don't want to ask anyone else because of the sensitive nature of the project. I see that it's 5:15 and I recall that you need to leave at 5:30 to pick up your children. Are you able to stay late? If not, can you pick them up, and come back with them to finish this very important assignment?"

If Edward had answered yes, then Cecelia could have proceeded: "Good. I need to call a Special Meeting of the Board of Directors tomorrow at 4:00 p.m. However, there is a catch—I need Bryan, Bethany, and Bob to attend, but not Karl or Karen."

"Please copy this 25-page document and overnight it to Bryan, Bethany, and Bob, with return receipt requested. Also, follow-up with calls to them tomorrow morning at about 11:00 to make sure they received the document and can attend. Edward, I gave you several instructions, and may have spoken a bit rapidly; please repeat what I asked you to do to make sure I was clear."

Cecelia would then know whether Edward had heard all of the steps and could proceed. If Edward didn't hear them all or did not understand what she wanted him to do, he could have asked, or she could have repeated the information.

Had Edward said "no" to the initial question about his ability to stay late, then Cecelia would have had numerous decisions to make: was there someone else she could trust with this assignment? Could she delay the special board meeting by one day and have Edward complete the assignment the following day? Or, could she come back after meeting with the outside consultant and complete the work herself? Any of those options would have been better than what happened.

Tips to Ensuring You Are Understood: Getting Another to Do What You Want

✓ Communicate to people in the manner they best take in information.

✓ Let her or him know what is to be achieved and the important role he or she will play.

✓ Repeat the desired result in the same or a different communication method "If you don't get them on the swings, get them on the merry-go-round...."

✓ Check for understanding.

✓ Show appreciation for a task well done.

✓ Show flexibility and a willingness to roll up one's sleeves and help.

② MAKE IT EASY FOR THEM TO SAY YES

In this chapter, we shift the focus to employee communication. How do employees get others to do what they want in the workplace without the clout of organizational superiority? Staff members have to do what the boss asks, but their bosses and peers don't have to do likewise.

President Ronald Reagan often quoted the Russian proverb, "Trust but verify," in reference to communication practices. He also instilled a discipline in his staff, requiring them to submit their written concerns on a single sheet in 4 points: issues, facts, reasoning, and recommendations. Borrowing both of these practices, I would also advise: make it easy for the recipient to say yes.

When employees need to ask their bosses or peers to do something, their requests are often incomplete. A memo or presentation might set out an issue and a desired result but fails to communicate what it takes to accomplish the job.

Even if the request is approved, without a concrete plan to complete it, often nothing happens. Typically, this isn't because the decider's intent isn't noble. The decision-maker is often a very busy person with other many other matters on his plate. The intent is pure, but the time and ability to ensure it gets done is missing. "Best laid plans of mice and men..."

The How To's

1. Present the problem, issue, or concern to be addressed.

2. Discuss the importance of the project.

3. Present all of the alternatives that were considered.

4. Present the selected option and the reasoning behind the selection.

5. Detail who will need to do what.

6. Set the timeline and detail the necessary resources.

7. Accept responsibility for the project's resolution or completion.

8. Don't make plans for others to complete unless they have agreed to do so beforehand.

9. Be equipped to answer all questions posed; anticipate the questions and know the facts.

10. Write it down on one sheet of 8-1/2 x 11" paper. (Remember Ronald Reagan.)

Case Study 2.1

Approximately 30% of a large manufacturing firm is comprised of baby-boomers who are eligible for retirement and will be gone from the company in three to five years. A cross-functional team of in-house executives developed a plan to train incoming and newly hired employees by creating a series of YouTube videos that feature incumbent employees in one-of-a-kind jobs.

The PowerPoint presentation to the CEO and his senior staff identified the issues: the potential loss of many employees in one-of-a-kind jobs; the need to have training materials on hand; and the relatively minor cost associated with the YouTube solution. The presentation contained dynamic graphics and bells and whistles and featured a sample video. It concluded that the videos would be created in-house. Hard copy videos could be kept in the company's library, where employees who did not have access to the Internet could check them, and virtual videos would be accessible through the company's intranet.

However, there was a catch: no one on the team had time to create the videos, nor did anyone work in the company's library. On top of this, no one on the team had budgetary control.

The CEO and his senior team thought the solution was innovative and would be great and agreed to support the project.

Although developing videos was a terrific solution, even with enthusiastic support from the CEO, nothing has been done to date.

What Went Wrong?

1. The necessary parties were consulted but no commitments were made. The individuals who could create the videos were busy with other company priorities and could not carve out the time to do so. Similarly, the in-house library staff was unavailable, and the IT department was focused on a new customer service system.

   Further, the development team neglected to ask for budgetary control or the ability to acquire additional resources such as employees, contractors, and consultants.

CONSEQUENTIAL COMMUNICATION IN TURBULENT TIMES

2. The company was restructuring and the library did not have the resources to accommodate the request—they could neither store the hard copy videos, nor assist employees in checking them out.

3. No person or function was assigned to determine which of the existing positions were most at risk of knowledge loss due to the retirements. Thus, there was no one to identify which videos should be made, or in what order.

Key Elements

Ensuring That It's Easy to Say Yes

1. Identify the issue, concern, or problem to be solved and their importance to the organization. Be strategic.

2. Discuss the importance of finding a solution to the issue, concern, or problem.

3. Develop alternative solutions to be considered.

4. Identify the selected alternative and provide the reasoning.

5. Develop a timeline and a budget, and outline the people and resources needed.

6. Ensure that the requester will accept full responsibility for the implementation, and that others needed to work on this project can make it a priority.

7. Think through the entire process associated with each alternative from "soup to nuts" (beginning to end); identify all of the possible questions that need to be answered and answer them.

8. Document the plan on a single sheet.

9. Do it!

"Making it easy for the decision-makers to say yes," means thinking through the entire process—from soup to nuts—and then accepting responsibility for its implementation.

Case Study 2.2
A Presentation That Worked

To meet the demands of a rapidly growing town, a builder in a formerly sleepy California suburb was faced with having to increase her company by 1/3, or from 200 to 300 employees. The Company has a great reputation, but if it doesn't grow to meet the increased building demands, the work will go to other companies.

To meet the challenge, the CEO asked the human resources department, which consists of a manager and two staff members, to present a plan to increase the company's workforce.

Following the steps outlined, the HR team made a PowerPoint presentation to the owner and her top lieutenants and followed it up with a document reduced to one 8½ by 11" sheet of paper. The presentation, with slides mapping to the key elements on the previous page follows.

Slide Show Presentation

Slide #1: Issue

Slide #2—Importance to the Company

Script Followed: In alignment with the strategic plan, the Company is experiencing dramatic growth, which will include expanding from 200 to 300 full-time employees. It is critical that HR be able to recruit, hire, train, compensate, and retain the right employees for the right jobs.

Slide #3—Alternatives Considered

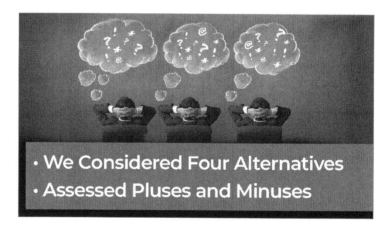

Script Followed: The department considered 1) expanding its current staff to meet the growing needs; 2) outsourcing the recruitment, hiring and on-boarding to an external consulting firm; 3) using consultants to "rifle-shot" in, when needed; and, 4) using temporary employees for the next six months.

Slide #4—Alternative Selected and Why

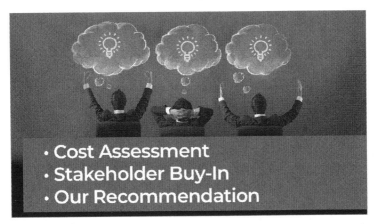

Script Followed: We carefully considered all of the options. We focused on the Company's goals, the costs associated with each alternative, and the availability of the internal and external resources. In addition, we discussed these options with the departments that will hire the majority of the new employees, construction and property. At the end of the process, we determined that hiring two additional full-time HR employees will allow the company to best achieve its overall goal of increasing the workforce, and to remain the leader in the competitive construction business.

Slide #5—Process for Moving Forward

Script Followed: Once we have approval for the plan, the HR department will recruit and hire the two new employees. The team will conduct skill-based interviews and the hiring panels will include representatives from construction and property, the departments that will experience the majority of the growth. We need their buy-in.

The two new HR employees will be on-board within two months. The two salaries will total $150,000. That along, with the 20% benefit cost, will total $180,000. HR has space and furniture in the department; IT has equipment on-hand, and there is sufficient parking.

Slide #6—Roles and Responsibilities

Script Followed: HR is prepared to move on this immediately. The construction and property departments have agreed to participate in the recruitment, hiring, and onboarding of the two new employees. HR also has approval from IT to install the computer equipment and from the Admin group to assign parking spots and reconfigure the furniture we have.

Slide #7—Questions

Because the team had done its homework—it thought through the likely questions—they were ready to answer on the spot. As anticipated, the first question came from the CEO who expressed surprise at the cost and wondered what the costs of the other alternatives were.

Script Followed: The manager stated, "After securing bids from outside consulting firms, it would cost $250,000 to outsource the hiring function and our internal staff would still be called upon to do much of the work. To 'rifle-shot' in experienced consultants would cost $150,000, and we would still need staff to dedicate to the company's growth over the long-term. Temporary employees could be used; we would hire two at a cost of $50,000.00 each, for a total of $100,000. Although this would be less expensive in the short-run than hiring two full-time employees and expanding the human resources function, it would free up the time of the three incumbents to work on more strategic matters above and beyond the transition to the new workforce."

Slide #8—Summary Plan

Script Followed: In conclusion, HR is here to support the strategic growth of the company. After considering numerous alternatives to enable the team to increase the company's size by 100 employees, or a full 1/3 of the current workforce, we recommend you give us the budget to hire two, full-time employees to get the job done. We have the support of the other departments that we need to collaborate with—construction, IT and property.

A Tried-and-True Sample 8.5 × 11" Template: The Follow-Up Memo to the PowerPoint Presentation

Issue, Problem, or Concern

With the advent of hiring and integrating 100 new employees (1/3 of the employee population) into the workforce, the Human Resources Department needs to expand from three employees to five.

Alternatives Considered

After studying the matter, consulting with outside companies similar to ours that have undergone dramatic increases in hiring, and relying upon the expertise in the human resources associations we belong to, the human resources department explored the following four alternatives:

1. Hire two new employees.
2. Outsource the recruitment, hiring, and employee onboarding process (integration) to a nationally-recognized consulting firm.
3. Bring in two independent contract experts in the field to manage the process.
4. Bring on two temporary employees full-time to manage the process for up to twelve months.

Selected Recommendation

After careful consideration of the alternatives, costing each of them out, and consulting with the client departments, we recommend hiring two new full-time human resources staff members to bring the function up to five, full-time employees.

The cost for this alternative, which includes salary, benefits, equipment, parking, and ancillary overheads are approximately $180,000, while using a nationally-recognized consulting firm would cost $200,000, two expert independent contractors (total $150,000), and two temporary employees would cost a total of $100,000.

All of the alternatives require the current staff to work with the adjunct staff. The benefit of hiring employees means that current staff can be redeployed to work on other critical people-related projects.

Roles and Responsibilities

Who Will Bear Responsibility and What is the Time Frame?

HR will need a mid-year budget adjustment upward of $180,000. We have consulted with the CFO who indicates there are moneys that can be transferred to HR from other functions. The departments within the company that will be impacted more than others—construction and property—have agreed to devote the time to participate in interviewing and onboarding the two new employees. Our goal is to commence recruitment and hiring within a week of approval.

Conclusion

The Company's HR department requests a mid-year budget increase of $180,000 to cover the costs of hiring two, full-time employees to assist with the recruitment and hiring of 100 additional employees to the company. Our recommendation is supported by our peers within the company who will be impacted most with the planned employee growth. They have agreed to participate as needed. With your approval today, we will commence the process this week.

Revisiting Case Study 2.1

Following the tried-and-tried template, think how this very good idea could have moved from approval to implementation.

Issue, Problem, or Concern

Baby-boomer employees comprise approximately 30% of our workforce. Some have begun to retire, and we anticipate that all or the large majority will be retired within three-to-five years. Of the 30% eligible for retirement, about half of them—or 15% of the total retirement-eligible population—have unique, one-of-a-kind jobs. We need to retrain current employees and to hire new ones to fill these positions.

Alternatives Considered

A Retirement Working Group was formed, with representatives from every department. The Group met over the course of three months. Members identified the possible retirements within their departments and the positions that would be left unfilled. They have also identified one-of-a-kind positions and internal employees that could be trained to fill those jobs. Finally, each department identified those positions for which they would hire from outside the Company.

The group, led by the Production Department, brain-stormed to come up with approximately 10 ideas, and then identified three possible solutions: 1) hire a consultant to develop a training program; 2) pair up those eligible for retirement with employees that plan to stay to with the Company, to pass along knowledge through hands-on-training via job shadowing; and 3) develop a series of YouTube videos depicting incumbent employees doing the work and explaining the process.

Selected Recommendation

After much discussion, which included going back to the drawing board several times, a consensus was finally reached, and the team recommended the development of employee YouTube videos, along with the employees describing what they were doing and why.

The cross-functional team considered that the costs to the Company involved both money and time. They also identified what internal capabilities exist for seeing the recommendation through to completion. After costing out the alternatives, the group determined that hiring a consultant to develop a training program would require a huge investment in money and time—bids ranged from $250,000 to $400,000 and productivity would decrease during the numerous employee interviews that each consulting firm would need to conduct.

The group determined that pairing up employees for one-on-one training through job shadowing would reduce productivity dramatically. Furthermore, there would be no way of determining that the employees trained would stay with the Company.

Roles and Responsibilities

Who Will Bear Responsibility and What is the Time Frame?

Miranda Ramirez from the Communications Department served as a representative on the working group. Everyone agreed that if approved by the department head, Communications should lead the project. They would work with

IT, who would place the videos on the Company's Intranet. Miranda was able to find both internal and thrifty external resources to complete the videos.

Department head Devon Washington approved the people request to complete the videos and cautioned that there were no moneys in the budget. Miranda went back to the working group, indicating $50,000 would be needed. Each department agreed to contribute up to $10,000 to the project.

Conclusion

To ensure smooth operation of the Company during the next three to five years, when approximately one-third of the workforce is eligible to retire, the Retirement Working Group recommends developing a series of You-Tube videos of employees explaining how to do their jobs. One-of-a-kind jobs that are currently filled by employees who are eligible for retirement will be prioritized. The videos will be placed on the Company's Intranet. The Communications Department will lead this effort, with buy-in from all departments where the videos will be shot. IT will upload the videos as they are created. At this time, no additional budget is requested. The Retirement Working Group will make quarterly reports. We request your approval.

Tips for Making it Easy for Them to Say Yes

✓ Recognize that the decision makers are busy people with multiple projects in front of them.

✓ To ensure success, anticipate and plan for all of the steps needed to complete the project.

✓ Be clear, concise, and thorough. And as it is oft said, "Be brief, be brilliant, be gone."

✓ Assume responsibility for execution.

✓ Do it!

3

THE PLATINUM RULE OF COMMUNICATION

Our motives are pure: All of us want to be understood, and we usually assume that we are. This is because we practice the "Golden Rule of Communication," meaning that we communicate with others the way we want to be communicated with. Wouldn't it be more effective to practice the "Platinum Rule of Communication"—to communicate with others the way *they* want to be communicated with?

People take in information in their own unique ways. Some people listen and "get it" the first time, while others need to listen to the same information multiple times, or in different ways. (If you don't get them on the slide, get them on the merry-go-round....) Some like to hear the information first, and then have it followed up in writing.

Some people read information once, while others need to read through it several times. Many people respond better to pictorial representations, graphs, diagrams, Excel spreadsheets, etc. In today's world, some gravitate towards electronic communication such as email and text. Online and social media options such as Google, Facebook, Instagram, and Twitter are also effective in helping people learn and connect.

As someone who needed to be in class (following the adage that it was better to "study the professor than the subject") and to hear what the professor had to say, I always found it frustrating that some students who never came to class could show up and ace the final exam. Clearly, those students got their information in alternative modes—reading the textbook, reading others' notes, purchasing CliffsNotes, or doing independent research.

To be effective leaders we need to understand how best to communicate with others. How do we do that?

The How To's

1. Ask what the person prefers.

2. Observe how they take in information.

3. Check for understanding in a group setting.

4. Check for understanding one-on-one.

5. If the person doesn't repeat the essence of the dialogue, follow-up with "I'm sorry, I wasn't very clear, let me try it again."

6. Try various methods and modes.

7. Flex your style.

1. **Ask what the person prefers.** Some people can tell you how they like information transmitted to them, though this is typically a small group.

2. **Observe how they take in information.** Become a keen observer of others. When participating in a meeting—particularly when conducting one—look for signs of understanding: nodding of heads and relaxed, even smiling faces—as opposed to crinkled brows and quizzical looks—and take note of the eager beavers who provide feedback through participation. Watch how others respond to them.

3. **Check for understanding in a group setting.** Many adults feel that seeking understanding from others is demeaning. Rather than ask "who wants to repeat what I just said?" seek volunteers to replay what was said or asked.

   If, after leading a group and having communicated the same information in multiple methods and modes, the trained facilitator continues to see more quizzical expressions than nodding heads, the response can be, "I think I just confused myself. Who thinks he or she understands what I was trying to say and can put it in his or her own words?" This works every time.

4. **Check for understanding in a one-on-one.** For leaders, a one-on-one typically involves giving an assignment or providing constructive feedback. In either case, it is critical that the recipient of the communication gets it. After all, the communicator wants the recipient to understand, act, and do what was requested. After engaging in dialogue, conclude with, "It's important to me that I was clear in what I said, so please summarize in your words what we talked about (or what I said, or what we agreed to, etc.)."

5. **If the person doesn't repeat the essence of the dialogue, follow-up with "I'm sorry, I guess I wasn't very clear, let me try it again."** Finally, when the recipient of the communication understands, follow up with "Do me a favor, send me a quick e-mail (or text) summarizing what you will do based upon our conversation."

6. **Try various methods and modes.** Try communicating verbally, in writing, by e-mail, and text, and be sure to follow-up. Always conclude by asking, "What questions do you have?" Posing the question this way, versus the standard "Do you have any questions?" creates an environment where questions are expected and natural. It removes the perception that anyone who has a question was "not paying attention, or is stupid." After all, the goal is to get the recipient to understand and then to do what we want.

7. **Flex your style.** Communication can be direct and straightforward, which often entails using the "w" words: "What do you think? What would you like me to do? What's your answer?" "Why should we do it that way? Why her and not me? Why not do it this way?" or "Which direction should we take?"

   Alternatively, communication can be indirect yet still fulsome. This often entails using the "h" word: "How might that work? How would you like me to do that?"

The trick is to figure out if the listener will respond better to the direct or the indirect method.

Think of brass instruments. For those who like the straightforward style of communication, let's call them trumpets. The thoughts go straight from the brain to the mouth in an immediate exhale/response. "W" questions typically work with trumpets.

For those who spend time to think before they speak, visualize the French horn. The player exhales and the breath goes around the tubing in a slow exhale/response. For the French horn players, the "w" statements can be intimidating, or at a minimum, off-putting. Try the "how" question.

Trumpeters communicating with French horn players should try to flex their style and adopt new phraseology. Rather than state "What do you think about this?" try a different approach: "How might this work?" "How about if we try it this way?" or "Do you have any initial thoughts on this?" Trumpet players will find that the French horn players will likely respond with an opening thought.

Likewise, French horn players who are being questioned by a trumpeter might try to flex their style and state, "My first thought is x; may I get back to you later?" or "Interesting question. I'm thinking of x and reserve the right to change with additional information." French horn players will realize that the trumpeters are often looking for preliminary thoughts or direction and are willing to allow for change after more study and information.

Case Study 3.1

Three supervisors were competing with one another for the managerial position that opened up in a leadership-focused governmental agency. The first candidate was a French horn—he was careful, studious, and wanted to have all the facts before deciding. In short, he hesitated to commit himself until he felt confident of his response.

The second candidate, after learning about what the job entailed, pulled out of consideration.

The third candidate was a trumpet—there was never an idea, or question that she didn't have a ready-made answer for, whether right or wrong. She could always change her mind when more facts were gathered, and then re-characterize her first response as just "thinking out loud, which no one should take seriously."

The coach for these candidates reported that the two were presented with a real-time issue by the hiring manager that they would encounter on the job and were given an opportunity to demonstrate how they would develop and execute a plan. When the issue was posed to both of them at the same time, the French horn was silent, while the trumpet immediately responded with a solution.

One week later, the French horn had a response, a roadmap to achieve the desired results, and had identified individuals who could achieve each part of the plan. The trumpet also had a plan that turned out to be different from her initial verbal solution. Neither plan was spot on, though both were workable. Arguably, the French horn's plan had been thought through more thoroughly and was more likely to be embraced by the new team of employees. Nonetheless, the trumpet was promoted.

What Went Wrong?

1. Whether "fair" or not, the trumpet was perceived as being "brighter, sharper, and more on top of things" because she gave an immediate response, even though her ultimate solution differed from that initial response. On the face of it, the decision-makers failed to allow for differing communication styles.

2. The decision-makers failed to seek understanding when posing the problem to be solved, which could have allowed for better responses.

3. None of the players perceived the best way to communicate with the others.

4. Had the manager who posed the question recognized the differing communication styles and flexed his own to accommodate the French horn player, perhaps the outcome would have been different.

Consider this: Following his coach's advice, the French horn agreed to flex his style in a way he felt comfortable, and to demonstrate that he "got it" by responding to a direct question or directions by stating "My initial thought is..." "We might try moving in this direction..." or "Subject to a bit of research, I think..." and following with "I'll get back to you with a fully formed response by...." Although the French horn didn't get the first job, by following his coach's advice, he nailed the second managerial opportunity.

In coaching the hiring manager, he agreed to flex his style in the future by tailoring the ask: "I don't expect you to have a fully formed solution right now; however, I'm interested in your initial thoughts. Get back to me/us in one week with your final thoughts."

By flexing one's style and trying to ferret out how best to communicate with the other parties, in the end the decision-makers make better decisions.

Case Study 3.2

Felicity and Jasmine each volunteer for a nationally recognized women's association that is committed to doing good works in their respective communities. The two were assigned to co-chair the annual fundraiser.

Felicity took in communication by hearing it the first time. She didn't need the information repeated, and when someone did, felt like "I'm not an idiot, why do they think they need to repeat?" If she occasionally got it wrong, it was no big deal.

Jasmine, on the other hand, took in information by listening to it carefully, and then reading follow-up notes or instructions. She wanted to ensure she "got it right," and didn't feel comfortable relying on information the first time she heard it.

The two started planning the event. Practicing the golden rule of communication, each communicated with the other the way she wanted to be communicated with. Thus, Felicity would say something once to Jasmine, never repeat herself, and expect that Jasmine would get it.

Jasmine, on the other hand, left each meeting, made meticulous notes, and then sent them to Felicity.

Each was upset with the other. Felicity confronted Jasmine stating, "Why do you keep sending me follow-up notes? Don't you think I get it the first time?" For her part, Jasmine was upset that Felicity never followed up with notes, thinking Felicity wouldn't follow up on what was agreed upon.

Both were well-meaning and good-intentioned but simply communicated with the other the way each wanted to be communicated with.

What if? At the beginning of the partnership, the two had a brief conversation along the lines of "what's the best way for us to stay in touch and to confirm what we've agreed to?" Felicity could have said "I'm fine with just discussing what we'll do once. I'll remember what I agreed to and do it. You can count on me." Jasmine could have said "I work best with follow-up notes. I have an idea. After we meet and decide what will happen next, I'll go ahead and write notes, so I can reference them. If you ever need them, let me know."

That short conversation would have set the agreed-to communication ground rules, avoided hurt feelings and anger, and both could have focused their attention on what they shared in common: raising money to enable the organization to fund community programs.

Tips for Practicing the Platinum Rule: Getting the Best Out of Others

✓ Determine how best the recipient will understand the communication. Ask how the recipient likes to receive information, observe, and/or try different methods and modes.

✓ Check for understanding.

✓ Flex one's style to meet the others' needs.

(4)

STRATEGIC COMMUNICATION

In his landmark book, *The 7 Habits for Managers,* one of the late Stephen Covey's habits was "Begin with the end in mind." Think about what the goal is, and then develop the path to achieve it. Simply stated: Be strategic.

Strategic communication is determining the goal to be achieved and planning the communication to achieve that objective. The aim could be the communication itself, such as "I want to communicate to Juanita the importance of completing the memo this afternoon." The communication could support a larger purpose for the organization, such as "I want Ruby Receptionist to mail out the appeal letters this evening, to ensure that the homeless agency can raise an additional $10,000 to provide needed services to our clients."

The How To's

1. Determine what the goal is.

2. Share the goal with those who play a part in achieving it.

3. Revisit the goal and adjust it, if necessary.

1. **Determine what the goal is**. This sounds easy, but defining the goal is crucial and often not thought through sufficiently. Spending time up-front thinking and formulating, consulting with others when appropriate, and testing the ultimate aim are all important components of determining the final goal. Said another way, "What does success look like? At the end of this (project, assignment, facilitation, communication, etc.) it will have been successful if *what* happens?"

2. **Share the goal with those who play a part in achieving it.** It is crucial to let those who will be involved in the project know what the objective is, and the important part they will play in attaining it. Employees who are in the know feel trusted and good about their contributions. They are more productive and can be relied upon to do their best work. Remember Ruby Receptionist from Chapter 1? Had she known the critical role she was playing to aid more homeless individuals, the story may have ended up quite differently.

   If it is not possible to share all the information associated with the goal, be honest and explain why. For instance, the boss could say to her assistant, "I need you to type up these notes to allow the organization to compete for an outside contract. Unfortunately, I am not in a position to share which contract it is. However, it is vital that these notes be typed up today, and with no errors. I'm giving you the assignment because I know the quality of your work, and your professionalism, and am confident you'll do a good job."

3. **Revisit the goal, and adjust it, if needed.** If things are off-track, was the initial communication clear, focused on the outcome, and understood? Did the communicator check for understanding? It's time to revisit the communication to ensure the goal was understood. If not, it's time to communicate again, using a different method or mode, and to check for understanding to ensure the communicator will get what she or he wants.

   If after checking to see that the communication was on target, and the product or process was inadequate from a timing perspective, or the quantity and quality of work completed was found wanting, it's time to revisit the goal to ensure it is the proper one, and to adjust it if necessary. If the objectives can be adjusted, do so and explain the rationale to all involved. If it can't be, double-down and engage those who need to participate more fully and power through to completion. It's time for the communicator (often the boss) to roll up his sleeves and help.

Here's an example of what to say when the goal can be adjusted: "I know we are all trying our hardest, but we have encountered unforeseen obstacles. I've reviewed our goal and am happy to report that I was unrealistic with my expectations. We can add another month to our schedule. This will allow me to meet with key players individually, and then together as a team to ensure we're all on the same page and doing our best work."

On the other hand, here's an example of what can be communicated when the goal cannot be adjusted: "I know we are trying our hardest and have encountered unforeseen obstacles. I've reviewed our goal with an eye towards adjusting the time frames. Unfortunately, we can't do that and still achieve the overall objective; it turns out that the project is more time sensitive than I thought. So, I'm removing other tasks from your plates and will work with you to ensure the duties associated with our goal are prioritized. I'll also be working with each of you directly to make sure we're on track and will authorize overtime."

Case Study 4.1

Remember Cecelia CEO from Chapter 1? Her overarching goal was to hold a special meeting of the majority of the Board of Directors the following day, with the purpose of voting two members off the board for having engaged in ethical violations. Her strategic goal with Executive Assistant Edward was to get him to complete the administrative work associated with mailing out the meeting notices to the three board members who needed to attend, to ensure they had the materials in advance and were able to attend.

In the end, Edward mailed out the three notices, but sent one, unfortunately to one of the board members that Cecilia wanted to vote off the board. Further, he put the materials in the regular mail rather than the over-night mail, and he didn't ensure that the look and feel of the materials were as professional as they might have been. Clearly, he didn't read the materials because he did not confirm attendance of those invited nor did he ready the boardroom. Finally, he left the documents in the copier, allowing the office gossip to find them and spread the news throughout the organization. The fiasco that followed ended with both Cecelia and Edward losing their jobs.

What Went Wrong?

Cecilia CEO had not thought through sufficiently her goal. For instance, was it critical that the Special Board Meeting be held the following day, or was it more important that the Meeting be planned, that no errors be made, and that Executive Assistant Edward have more time to set it up?

Cecilia did not share the goal with Edward and his important role in completing his part on time and as professionally as possible. Had she explained that the materials to be sent were required to call for a special meeting the following day, and explained that they must be sent out overnight with return receipt requested, Edward likely would have done so.

Cecilia did not check for understanding; she took Edward's nod as understanding. Had she explained that the materials to be sent were required to call for a special meeting the following day and explained that they must be sent out overnight with return receipt requested, Edward likely would have done so. If Cecilia CEO did not feel able or comfortable sharing this confidential information with Edward, she could have said, "Edward, I am not at liberty to explain why, but it is critical that only Bryan, Bethany, and Bob receive this information. Karl and Karen are *not* to receive this information, nor are you authorized to read it. Please check to make sure these directions are followed."

Consider this: At 5:00 p.m., Cecilia CEO learned from a private investigator that two of her five outside board members were selling proprietary company documents to a competitor. This information confirmed her suspicions. After reading the detailed report, Cecilia CEO called the investigator to set up a 5:45 p.m. meeting off-site with her Company lawyer to learn more, and to see what her legal options were.

Out of anger and disgust, Cecilia CEO wanted the two "traitors" off the board immediately and thought calling a special meeting of the balance of the board the following day at 4:00 p.m. to vote the three off should do the trick.

Recognizing that when she had acted hastily out of anger in the past, her decisions had not always been in the best interest of the Company or herself, she considered whether to call the meeting for the next day, or whether she should wait a day or two. Cecilia called her outside adviser, a long-standing friend whom she trusted, who agreed that time was of the essence, and Cecilia should call for a 4:00 p.m. meeting on the following day.

At the decision-point, it was 5:10 p.m. and Cecilia drafted a handwritten cover note to each of the three board members she would like to attend the special meeting. She called in her Executive Assistant at 5:15 p.m. to copy the 25-page report and overnight it to Bryan, Bethany, and Bob.

Recalling that Edward Executive Assistant was a single parent who needed to leave at 5:30 p.m. to pick up his children from daycare, the conversation could have gone as follows: "Edward, it's 5:15, and I recall that you need to leave at 5:30 to pick up your children from daycare. I have an extremely important assignment that could take up to ½ hour, are you able to stay late to do so?"

Edward, somewhat embarrassed that he hadn't yet put Plan B into place, indicated "no," he must leave at 5:30. Cecilia CEO readjusted, and advised Edward that she would not delay the Special Board Meeting; rather it would be held the following day at 4:00 p.m.

Because Edward would leave soon, Cecelia needed him to type up three labels for overnight delivery to Board members Bryan, Bethany, and Bob, and to prepare three envelopes large enough to accommodate a 25-page confidential document in the next 15-minutes. Cecilia indicated that she would make the copies and walk them to the drop-off in front of the building on her way out.

She also confided in Edward that other than herself, he was the only person she trusted to work on important confidential matters relating to the Company. Further, tomorrow he should call the three at 11:00 a.m. to confirm their attendance in the Company boardroom at 4:00 p.m., and he would need to prepare the room.

Cecilia also stated, "Edward, I know that I advised you during the job interview that we are a family-friendly company, and I do understand your need to leave by 5:30 to pick up your children. I also advised you that from time-to-time, I would need you to stay late. Normally, I would have advance notice. Unfortunately, tonight I did not. This is a highly unusual situation. However, since it could happen again in the future, please make sure you have alternative arrangements for pickup from childcare. Thank you."

Cecelia called the investigator and Company lawyer and pushed the meeting back to 6:00 p.m., copied the documents, stuffed the envelopes and took them to the pick-up spot before leaving.

The following day she reminded Edward to confirm attendance by calling Bryan, Bethany and Bob at 11:00 a.m. and to prepare the boardroom for the meeting. Cecilia told Edward that two outside guests would be coming, and he should plan for them also. She also reminded Edward to work on plans for childcare coverage for those few times he would be expected to work late.

Tips for Strategic Communication

✓ "Begin with the end in mind." What is the goal to be achieved with the communication?

✓ Develop tactics to support the strategy. What needs to be done to achieve the strategic objective?

✓ Work backwards from the goal.

✓ Ensure that all others involved are informed and understand what their respective roles are.

5

LISTENING, ASKING, AND TELLING

Verbal communication consists of listening, asking, and telling. Far too many of us do too much telling and too little listening and asking—especially bosses. We are comfortable with problem solving and telling those who report to us what to do and how to do it.

As leaders we were promoted to our lofty positions because we were great individual contributors. We saw an issue or situation, analyzed it, developed solutions, and implemented. We took initiative with confidence and without fear, and we were rewarded for it.

Doing all of the "telling" robs those who report to us of the ability to grow and develop. It also serves as a disincentive for employees to take the initiative to identify concerns and solve problems. Additionally, it deprives the leader of learning that there might be a better idea than the one she or he developed.

Managing and leading require different skill sets than those of the great individual contributor. These skill sets don't necessarily come naturally or easily. Who teaches the boss how to coach, counsel, manage, lead, and to create an environment where people feel comfortable bringing forth their best ideas? If a leader does all of the following over a sustained period of time, the employee group will be motivated and dare to take risks. It can take a while for employees to see that their leaders' actions follow their words, but it will be worth it. After all, motivated employees are productive employees!

The How-To's

1. State the issue, concern, obstacle, or problem that needs to be solved, and ask "who has an idea on how we might proceed?"

2. Create a ground rule that you will be last to speak.

3. Take the sting or embarrassment out of a "dumb" idea by announcing there are no "dumb or stupid ideas."

4. Thank the first brave soul for his or her courage in daring to stand out, and acknowledge how hard that is.

5. Announce that everyone makes mistakes, and that an idea that leads to a mistake is okay so long as it's thoughtful, the person learns from it, and is willing to share it with others so they don't make the same one.

6. Listen, ask follow-up questions, ask others to add to the thought, and share what they think.

What Leaders will Learn

1. Someone who reports to you might have already thought of your "very excellent idea," and should be given the chance to express it.

2. Someone who reports to you might have a better idea.

3. The interactive process—the group give and take—might net a good or even an excellent idea that hasn't yet surfaced.

4. Issues, concerns, obstacles, or problems that the leader was not aware of might emerge.

5. Solutions to those previously unknown issues, concerns, obstacles, or problems might also emerge. In short, an unknown problem might be solved.

Case Study 5.1

Having made a "meteoric rise" in a large, investor-owned utility, an up-and-comer 38-year-old female lawyer was elected corporate secretary both to the utility and to its holding company. The department was comprised of a governance group numbering four—to handle the monthly board of director meetings, and shareholder services, a group of about 35 that handled stock purchases, dividend reinvestment, stock transfers, escheatment, etc.

The monthly board meetings were a fire drill, with the Corporate Secretary gathering reports from the CEO, various departmental vice presidents, and others, and editing them into short items that non-utility board members could easily understand. Adrenaline was flowing, the CEO changed his mind frequently, which caused work re-dos and work-arounds. The Secretary was a single mother that needed to leave on time or hire others to act in her stead. The monthly board "fire drill" exercise took up an entire week each month.

The Secretary wasn't interested in how the stock was doing, so she focused her time in between board meetings elsewhere. Fascinated by what motivated people and how to get the most out of them she was ready to experiment to inspire the team to do more, so she established self-managed work teams. After all, she had been promoted rapidly (five jobs in eight years) because she was known as a successful change agent. Throughout her utility career, the Secretary had been eager to establish these teams and had found her opportunity.

The Company held its annual meetings off-site in a toney hotel, and although most of the employees were shareholders, they were discouraged from attending. The meeting was was held during work hours. During one of these annual meetings, the proverbial "little old lady from Pasadena" stood up to complain to the CEO that she had received multiple annual reports. It was a waste of money for anyone to receive more than one of those glossy tomes and what was he going to do about it? The CEO and Corporate Secretary were the only two individuals seated on the dais. The commentary prompted a "if looks could kill" moment from the CEO to the Secretary.

After he glared at the Secretary, the CEO promised the problem would be solved. The Secretary had been unaware of this problem and knew that the look from the CEO meant "Never embarrass me again. Fix the problem."

This was the moment the Secretary was waiting for: an assignment that the self-managed work teams could solve! The day after the annual meeting, the Secretary called an all-hands meeting and relayed what had happened.

A brave soul in the assembled group raised her hand and said, "Oh yeah, we know that happens." When asked why, she stated, "Well, when someone calls up, we ask what his or her name is. We input the name into the system, and provide the service requested, be it a stock question, a purchase, or a dividend reinvestment. Because people call frequently, there are multiple variations on an individual's name in the system. So, each name is treated as a different person and gets an annual report." By way of example, Joseph Adam Smith could be in the system as: Joseph Adam Smith, Joseph A. Smith, J.A. Smith, or Joe Smith, among others. It all depends upon how he identified himself when he called in.

The Secretary thought to herself that it would be an easy fix: Just find a unique identifier for each person. In her mind, it would be the Social Security number.

Rather than give her opinion, the Secretary set up three, self-managed work teams. The first was to discuss alternatives and make a recommendation on how to solve the problem going forward. The second team was charged with determining how to clean-up the current, rather large, database. The third team was to implement the agreed-to solution. Each team was given its marching orders, as follows.

Process

1. Brainstorm the issue. Gather the team together and have an "anything goes" brainstorming session.

2. Narrow the brainstorming to three to five of the best ideas.

3. Test each idea by asking what the positives would be and what the negatives, or potential pitfalls might be.

4. Assign different team members to research the positives and negatives.

5. Reconvene in a week's time, allowing each team to present its research and recommendation.

6. Based upon a team discussion of the research, decide upon a recommendation.

To get the process started, each team should:

1. Select roles and responsibilities, recognizing that one person could play multiple roles: a) a team leader; b) the moderator or facilitator of the group brainstorming session; c) the notetaker; d) timekeeper; and, e) group coach, or the person who will stay in contact with each team member to answer questions, provide assistance, and ensure they are doing their part on time, within budget, etc.

2. Schedule dates and time frames for the brainstorming session and follow-up meetings, recognizing that the report back (due date) to the larger group is one week's time.

3. Determine what resources would be needed, e.g., time, treasure, and expertise.

4. Identify any ground rules that need to be established, such as how to handle a team member asking for assistance.

5. Develop a "Plan B" to account for any unforeseen events, for instance, a team member unable to fulfill the agreed-to task or role.

6. Document the work using the tried-and-true, single-sheet template discussed in Chapter 2 (the Ronald Reagan Rule):

- Present the problem, issue, or concern to be addressed.
- Discuss its importance to the organization.
- Present the alternative results considered.
- Present the alternative selected, and the reasoning behind it.
- Detail who will need to do what.
- Detail the time line and resources needed.
- Accept responsibility for its resolution or completion.
- Don't make plans that others need to complete unless they have agreed to do so beforehand.
- Be equipped to answer all questions posed
- Write it down on one sheet of 8 ½ × 11" paper.

Results

The following week, the entire group reconvened, with the first self-managed work team making its presentation. After the spokesperson introduced her team, identifying the role each member played, she began the presentation:

> "The issue to resolve is to send only one annual report per shareholder. To do this, we must find a way to consolidate the various names we have listed for each shareholder. Our team decided to tackle two issues. The first

was to look forward, and determine how we can stop this in the future. The second is to handle the current problem of one shareholder receiving multiple annual reports.

It is important to rehabilitate the department's stature with the CEO, and to avoid angering shareholders.

We discussed that we could avoid this in the future by assigning a single identifying feature to each shareholder. For those from the past, we decided we would have to determine which names belong to which accounts in order to consolidate them.

For the future, we discussed identifying individual shareholders by using their addresses, drivers' licenses, Social Security numbers, or by creating a unique pin. To address the current shareholders, we would need to get IT to assist us to consolidate as many as we can using the address, and then to contact those remaining. We discussed writing letters or calling them.

We also selected creating a unique pin. People move, so addresses and drivers' license numbers change. We could also use Social Security numbers, so our group took a vote and the unique pin won out.

For the current shareholders, we agreed we had better call all of those remaining (after the IT clean-up), so we can answer any questions the shareholders might have.

The IT Manager said he would need to study the database and could offer us two of his staff to work full-time on the consolidation. He could also help us to establish a system of unique pin numbers to assign for the future.

It will take IT three months with two people working full-time to clean up the system, and to develop and train us on the use of the unique pin numbers. We will then need two months to implement the plan.

I will accept responsibility for working with the IT Manager and his team and keeping you (Corporate Secretary) abreast of any slippage in the timeline. Team member Javier will accept responsibility for the training of all staff. He will also keep you apprised of any time frame slippage."

Questions

When the Corporate Secretary asked why the team didn't want to use Social Security numbers since it would reduce the process by eliminating the need to develop the unique pin numbers, the presenter stated, "Some people on the team were afraid they might input the wrong Social Security number when on the phone with the shareholder. Others thought our shareholders wouldn't want to give their Social Security numbers over the phone."

When the Corporate Secretary, who secretly had decided that using the Social Security number would work best, then asked, "Can't the Social Security number be verified in writing?" The presenter started to backtrack and indicated she would go back to the team for further discussion. When asked, she said she would get back to the Corporate Secretary in one week.

The day proceeded with teams two and three coming up with essentially the same information.

What Next?

Team one took a second vote and again voted for the unique pin. Because they were concerned that the Corporate Secretary didn't agree with them, team one members lobbied teams two and three to agree to back them up. Team one returned the following week and advised the Corporate Secretary that all three teams agreed that the unique pin would be best.

What Did the Corporate Secretary do?

Despite her strong belief that the Social Security number was the best solution (after all, banks, health care providers, and others used Social Security numbers for identification, why couldn't her department, she reasoned), she knew that by substituting her own "very good idea" for that of the hard working teams, she would defeat her own efforts to empower the workforce, and lose all credibility with the team. In a single action, she would prove herself an "old fashioned" boss that said, "I say jump, you ask how high?" so, she sucked it up and agreed to the unique pin numbers.

With the passage of time, when identity theft was on the rise, banks, health care providers, and others dropped the use of Social Security numbers and went to unique pins, the former Corporate Secretary chuckled to herself since she had proved her own point: Others had a better idea than she had!

End of This Tale

The staff became motivated, energetic, and took the initiative to identify other problems with the current system that needed to be rectified. One was escheatment, the system in California whereby unclaimed moneys go to the State. A small and mighty team raised this issue to the Corporate Secretary and provided a solution to the problem. Although it likely cost more money to track down the (usually former) shareholders or their heirs and to write a check, the staff was on a roll and the Secretary gave her go-ahead.

Moral of the Story

We should all do far more listening and asking, rather than telling, and we should "practice what we preach." You guessed it; it was I who was that Corporate Secretary.

Case Study 5.2

The Audit VP in a large Aerospace firm was pleased to have been hired into one of his client companies. Formerly a partner in a large auditing firm, Mel never felt comfortable in the linear, quiet, predictable world of auditors. By nature, he was outgoing, gregarious, people-oriented, and a risk-taker.

In his new position, Mel had a staff of 15 internal auditors, and joyously held a series of off-site meetings, focusing on team building, communication, and strategic planning.

Mel hired a trained facilitator to lead the group through a series of exercises that included the completion of a workplace team-building and communications assessment.

Mel was devastated to learn that his staff faulted him for not listening to their suggestions. The feedback indicated that although he asked for the opinions of his staff, more often than not he did what he wanted. In short, he was asking, but not listening, and certainly, he was telling.

As it turned out, the very thing Mel prized most in his new environment—the ability to brainstorm and solve problems with others—was his downfall. It turned out that Mel's style was to think out loud. When he asked for others' opinions, he often had a nearly formed idea about what to do, and was looking for confirmation.

The Solution

Mel agreed to do some soul-searching before speaking, and to state his intentions. During the retreat, the Audit team developed, and he agreed to, the following three ground rules:

1. If he really didn't have an idea about how to proceed, he would state "Team, I need your best ideas; I haven't the first idea about how to proceed."

2. If he had a sense of what he wanted to do, and was looking either for confirmation, or a better approach, he would say, "I am half-of-the way there, and am thinking this is the direction I'll take. I want your feedback, and if someone has a better idea, let's adopt it."

3. If Mel were 99% there and only wanted to hear if someone foresaw a huge problem that he didn't, he would say "Okay, team, I'm almost 100% there. However, if anyone can see that I'm about to walk into a buzz-saw, tell me now."

Result

By adopting these ground rules, within six months, Mel and his team were back on track. The team knew how much work to invest—almost none if Mel were 99% there, and a fair amount of time if he were unclear as to how to proceed. Finally, Mel had the team and the work environment that had he worked to attain for his entire career!

Tips for Listening, Asking, and Telling

✓ Listen and ask more, tell less.

✓ Announce your intentions by reflecting upon—and sharing—why you are asking.

✓ Adopt Mel's ground rules: When you seek input from others, determine whether you are almost there. Do you simply need confirmation? Do you need all good ideas? What will you do with them—will you implement them?

✓ If those you asked developed a solution that will work, do not substitute your "very good solution" for theirs (remember the Corporate Secretary).

6

"I" STATEMENTS AND "ACTS AND FACTS"

"You didn't understand." "You're not listening to me." "What you need to understand is..." "You didn't answer my question."

How many times have each of us heard one of those statements, or variations on the theme in the workplace, and usually coming from the boss? They might as well add "...you idiot, or you moron," since that's what it feels like.

How effective and more productive it would be if the boss said, "I'm sorry, I didn't explain well enough, here goes." Or, "I don't think I'm making my point, let me try it this way." Or, "I am even confusing myself with all of these explanations; please tell me what you think I'm trying to say."

Using "I" statements clearly places the responsibility where it lies: with the communicator.

It may sound radical, however: "It's not your job to understand me; it's my job to make myself understood." Ponder that one for a while.

Accepting responsibility for being understood fundamentally changes the communication dynamic from "you need to understand me," to "I need to communicate in a manner so that I am understood."

Typically, we make a statement, assume we are clear as the proverbial bell, and if someone else doesn't understand, it's his or her problem, not ours.

That never gets us very far, if we agree that when we communicate in the workplace, we're usually trying to get someone else to do what we want her or him to do. Thus, it's the communicator's problem.

The Impact of Using "You" Statements

"You didn't understand." "You're not listening to me." "What you need to understand." The recipient of those sentences can feel a range of emotion (never positive ones) from hurt, to anger, to humiliation, to being unworthy. Those statements can also have the effect of causing the recipient to become defensive and strike back. Worst of all—given that we want him or her to do something— the person is not disposed to want to try again.

The Impact of Using "I" Statements

Try "I'm sorry, I didn't explain well enough, let me try again," "I don't think I'm making my point, let me try it this way," or "I am even confusing myself with all of these explanations; please tell me what you think I'm trying to say."

The recipient of those sentences can feel a range of emotion from confusion to relief—"thank goodness it's not me"—to understanding. These are all preferable to hurt, anger, or humiliation. They can also produce the positive result of the recipient wanting to listen and learn, to be eager to help and willing to give it another try.

Example: Media Interviews

It can be intimidating to be interviewed live in front of an audience without knowing what the questioner will ask. Increasingly, interviewees often have a story they want to tell, regardless of the question. The questioner is often simply a vehicle used to allow the interviewee to state whatever she or had planned to say.

In turn, frustrated interviewers often fall into the "you" trap, stating, "You didn't answer my question." From the audience's point of view, this assertion can appear aggressive or intimidating. This could have the impact of the audience identifying with the interviewee, and giving him or her a pass on the question.

A few masterful interviewers respond with an "I" statement: "I didn't hear an answer to my question." In contrast, the interviewer has deftly pointed out that the interviewee has avoided the question. This can have the result of the audience thinking, "Oh yeah, why is he or she avoiding the question? Is there something to hide?" In addition, it's a statement of fact, "I didn't hear an answer to my question," rather than a conclusion or opinion.

Using Acts and Facts Rather than Conclusions, Opinions, or Attribution of Motivation

This is an extension on the maxim of using "I" statements vs. "you" statements.

"You didn't understand me," "You're not listening to me," "What you need to understand is…" "That was unprofessional," "You are behaving inappropriately," "You're getting angry," "You think that just because the boss picked you…"

All of those statements are conclusions, opinions, and/or attributions of motivation. They are not "acts or facts."

Reworking all of these, and focusing on acts and facts vs. conclusions, opinions, or attribution of motivation could produce:

FROM	TO
You didn't understand me.	I guess I wasn't clear, how about…
You're not listening to me.	It looks like I'm not being clear, let me try it this way…
What you need to understand is…	I'd really like to make this point since it will be important to the project.
That was unprofessional. OR You are behaving inappropriately.	The team's weekly meetings start at 9:00 a.m. sharp. I noticed you arrived at 9:15 a.m., knocked over chairs in the back row, and spoke over one of the team members. Those actions are inconsistent with our values. Please refrain in future.
You're getting angry.	I don't think this is a good time to have this conversation. How about we schedule a meeting for tomorrow at 11:00 a.m.?
You think that just because the boss picked you…	Wow, the boss picked you for this assignment. I know I'd be thinking about it this way. Are you interested?

One should always avoid speaking for the employee, or putting words in his or her mouth. How does anyone else know what the other understands or feels, or what motivates them? What if the person was listening and the communicator was unclear? Be concise about what was done or not done, and how someone can improve.

Let's face it—we all have opinions, draw conclusions, and even attribute motivations to others. It's not if we do this, it's rather whether we act on them.

What are the consequences of acting on our opinions and conclusions, and attributing motivations to others? At best, miscommunication, and at the worst, conflict, or sadly, in this day and age, violence.

The former CEO Cecelia assumed that Executive Assistant Edward knew an entire list of things: a) that he could stay late to do a last-minute assignment; b) that everything going to the board must be near perfection and overnighted return receipt requested; c) that he would read the materials and therefore know which board members should receive them, d) that he would always follow-up with a call; and, e) that he understood all of her instructions. From Cecelia's point of view, she was clear, and Edward just didn't get it.

Case Study 6.1

A board of directors of a local credit union had been intact for a number of years and everyone felt comfortable with one another. The credit union was in transition from its then current structure to becoming a community bank. Three new board members were added, each of whom had expertise in a needed area.

One new member was Carl Controller, who was a "numbers guy." As it turned out, the credit union had lost two controllers in quick succession and desperately needed to hire another to assist in the transition. Carl mentioned to the CEO at a board meeting that he knew a couple of good controllers in transition, and offered to connect them so the credit union could set up interviews. The CEO hired one of the referrals, Nydia Numbers.

Later, the CEO hired an outside consultant to assist with the transition and build a strong team, integrating the three new board members into the group. The consultant, Penelope, had a PhD in Organizational Behavior, and administered a modified "360-degree performance evaluation." A "360" is comprised of feedback from oneself, and their boss, peers, and subordinates. Since the feedback was coming from the individual about him- or herself and then from the peers, it was a modified 360.

The day that Penelope PhD was scheduled to give Carl Controller his feedback, she suggested they meet in the bar at a local hotel and chat over a drink. Naturally, this signaled to Carl that the feedback would be negative. Over two beers, Penelope advised Carl "your peers think you are manipulative." Carl, who was a seasoned 360-degree participant smiled, which was not the response Penelope expected.

When asked why, Carl stated, "Penelope, have you ever taken a 360-degree yourself?" She was taken aback and answered "no." He then stated, "I have taken and given these assessments over the years, and I would never tell anyone what you just said to me.

"Telling someone that he or she is manipulative is not useful. It could be viewed as hurtful or derogatory, and it doesn't assist the receiver in understanding what she or he did that could be improved upon in the future. I would want to know the 'acts and facts' behind the conclusion and attribution of motivation."

Penelope allowed as how one of the board members thought that Carl had recommended the new Controller to the credit union so that he could really run the department behind the scenes. Carl then let out a belly laugh and said, "That was the furthest thing from my mind. I was merely trying to help out. I've got enough on my plate at work to want to run another department. That tells me more about the person who made the statement than it does about me. It tells me that he or she would have recommended a hire in order to control things."

Although Carl's point of view was well-stated and well-reasoned, Penelope's comment put him on the defensive. This precluded his learning that in the future he might think twice before recommending someone for a job at an organization on whose board he sits. Or, at a minimum, to be aware of how his actions might affect others whose help he needs to work effectively as a team member.

This story ends with Carl leaving the board when the merger went through.

Why is dealing in acts and facts, not conclusions, opinions, or attribution of motivation a companion piece to using "I" statements? Both allow for the elimination of personal bias and assumptions about others, and both require personal responsibility of the communicator.

What if? Penelope had provided the acts and facts only. "Carl, you might want to be aware that when you recommended Nydia Numbers for the Controller position, some of your fellow board members drew the conclusion that you were trying to influence the department. As the new kid on the block, you might want to keep this in mind."

Might Carl had responded differently? Might the ending have turned out differently?

Tips for Using "I" Statements and Using Acts and Facts

✓ Assume responsibility for the communication. "I believe this," "I heard this," "I don't understand why this happened," "I observed," "I noticed," to state a few.

✓ Think and speak for the one person over which the communicator has control—yourself.

✓ State what happened or didn't happen neutrally. "I asked for the report to be turned in today by noon. I haven't seen it yet." "Some board colleagues think that you recommended a new finance manager so you could run the finance department." "I noticed that the meeting was cancelled, please tell me why."

✓ Avoid drawing conclusions, stating opinions, or attributing motives to others.

CHECK FOR UNDERSTANDING

"Assuming facts not in evidence" is one of many objections lawyers make in trial. It's not just television witnesses who fall prey to this; it happens to all of us. How many times has each of us said something that was perfectly clear in our own mind, yet the listener didn't understand? Could that be because the underlying facts are known by us, presumed accurate, and that we assumed "everybody knows that," or "everybody thinks that?"

Each of us attains a certain body of knowledge during our lifetime that comes from one or more of the following: 1) the unique work we have chosen; 2) the cultural heritage into which we were born or have selected; 3) our family unit or tribe; or 4) the family unit or tribe we decide we want to join, among others.

All of these groups have shared knowledge and experiences, which form the basis for their "assumed facts." As the world becomes progressively smaller, with diverse groups coming together in the workplace and society, it's increasingly more important to check for understanding. Simply stated, to check to ensure that the intent of the communication was understood.

In the workplace, it's vital to seek understanding to ensure that the receiver of the communication will do what is asked of him or her. None of us likes to ask for a project to be completed, only to find that the listener did something else. A simple shortcut to this dilemma is to follow this series of How To's to ensure understanding.

The How To's

1. *Ask: Please repeat back to me what I just said.*
2. *Seek follow-up.*
3. *Request a plan.*
4. *Hold follow-up-meetings.*
5. *Supervise the project.*
6. *Ensure the employee is capable of delivering.*

1. **Ask.** "Please repeat back to me what I just said (asked, wrote, e-mailed, or texted). I want to make sure I was clear."

2. **Seek follow-up.** "Great, to ensure we're on the same page, please go back to your office and jot me a quick e-mail stating what I've asked you to do."

3. **Request a plan.** "Now that we both understand what the finished product will look like, send me a timeline with bullet points so we can keep on track."

4. **Hold follow-up meetings.** "The timeline looks great. Let's hold a few more follow-up meetings to flesh it out a bit more—to see what resources you might need, to off-load some other work, and to make sure this is 'doable'."

5. **Supervise the project.** "Marisol, in reading your action plan, I see that you stated you would have completed the information gathering now. Are you on track? Great." If not, "Do you have an alternate date? Do you need assistance?"

6. **Ensure the employee is capable of delivering.** "Wow, I know this is a huge project, and I would find it hard to get it all done myself. Shall we ask others to join the team? If so, what parts do you feel best about completing? What parts should we ask others to help with?"

Case Study 7.1

Jacob was a compensation director for a large product development firm. The owner was eager to put in a "pay-for-performance plan" that would reward those who "shot the lights out of the park," and, hopefully, motivate others to do the same. The goal was to implement the plan by the beginning of calendar year 2019. Jacob was given the assignment in March 2018, which Calvin CEO thought was "ample time to get this done."

After several meetings between the two, Jacob put together a plan that consisted of the following:

- Survey what competitor companies were doing—March–April 2018
- Survey what other best-practice companies were doing—April–May 2018
- Research what the thought-leaders and futurists were recommending—May–June 2018
- Develop three alternative plans—June–August 2018
- Hold employee meetings to "test the waters"—August–September 2018
- Based on employee input, fine-tune proposed plans—late September 2018
- Present to the CEO and his C-Suite Team—October 2018
- Get Board approval—November 2018
- Launch in January 2019

There was no new compensation plan in place for 2019. What went wrong?

Jacob, who was well-meaning and good-intentioned had a tendency to "overcommit and underperform." Calvin CEO was marginally aware of this, but assumed Jacob would get the job done. After all, this was a high-profile project, so "of course he will bust his butt." Sadly, this was a case of "best laid plans of mice and men," and Jacob fell well behind, which in turn caused him to become discouraged, and, ultimately, to give up.

Jacob started like gangbusters, consulting with his colleagues in March and April to determine what others in his industry were doing. However, when the time came to consult with other best-practice companies, Jacob didn't know anyone personally at any of these companies and didn't know where to turn.

Embarrassed to show the big boss that he wasn't equipped to handle the project, Jacob instead muddled through. He researched what the thought-leaders in compensation were recommending, though most of the systems were designed for fast-growing tech firms, rather than more established development firms like the one Jacob worked for.

Pumped up by what the experts were saying, and falling behind schedule, Jacob did develop three alternative plans, all of which tracked what tech companies were doing. The alternatives weren't completed until September, which meant the employee meetings were held in October. Jacob thought he had made up time. He assumed the employees would buy-in, allowing him to stay on scheduled and present to the CEO and the C-Suite in late October.

In the employee meetings, Jacob was met with an array of questions he hadn't anticipated, concern over the changes he proposed, and anger over how these changes affected the workforce. The opinion leaders in the workforce stated things like, "This doesn't fit our industry," "Where did you get these ideas anyway?" "Why didn't you keep us informed earlier in the year?" and "If you take these to the CEO and the C-Suite, we will complain to them."

Sadly, by the time Jacob went back to the "drawing board," it was late fall 2018. There was no time for CEO and C-Suite approval, yet alone board approval.

What Went Wrong?   Calvin CEO completed the first three items on the checklist:

✓ He asked for understanding and sought follow-up (steps 1 and 2). Calvin held several initial meetings with Jacob, and then asked for a project timeline.

✓ He sought and received follow-up and he requested a plan (step 3). Jacob's timeline included all of the elements Calvin wanted, and he agreed to it.

✓ Where Calvin fell short was in the last three items.

He did not hold follow-up meetings. "The timeline looks great; let's hold a few follow-up planning meetings to flesh it out a bit more, to see what resources you might need, to off-load some other work, to make sure this is 'doable'."

Calvin failed to supervise the project. "Jacob, in reading your action plan, I see that you stated you would have completed the benchmarking against companies in our industry. I see that hasn't happened? I would be happy to help out. I can make a few calls if you like, or give you a list of contacts. What is needed here?"

His biggest error was in failing to ensure that Jacob was up to the task of delivering. "Jacob, this is a significant project and one I consider at the top of the priority list. It requires many tasks and duties, and I am not aware of whether this will be new or something you've done before. Will you need assistance? I'd like a ten-minute meeting each Friday to check in and see where we are."

Unfortunately, Calvin didn't work with Jacob to more fully outline the plan, nor did Calvin supervise the project or discover if Jacob was capable of delivering.

What if? Calvin had asked Jacob to provide a more fully detailed plan. For instance, a plan indicating who he would be contacting during the first three phases—which competitors, who at which best-practice companies, and which thought-leaders. What if Calvin or Jacob thought it would be better to hold employee meetings or send communications throughout the year to avoid the "surprise" factor?

What if Calvin had asked what other projects Jacob was working on that could be off-loaded to others, whether he needed assistance to complete the project, and whether he felt confident that he could deliver on all aspects of the plan? Last, what if Calvin had "managed by walking around," checking in with Jacob throughout to ensure he was on target?

Tips for Checking for Understanding

✓ Ask "I want to make sure I was clear. Please repeat what you understood me to say."

✓ Request confirmation. "Great conversation. Please go back to your office and e-mail me with how you plan to proceed."

✓ Manage by walking around. Check in to ensure the task, duty or project is on target.

✓ Off-load other work, when possible.

✓ Help, when needed.

8

THE TWO-FOR-ONE RULE, TIMING IS EVERYTHING, AND THE POWER OF POSITIVE FEEDBACK

"How many supervisors like to give performance feedback?" When this question was posed to over 500 leaders in one of the nation's largest municipal water and power companies, a scant few raised their hands. When asked to explain why, the answers boiled down to three responses: "Because I don't want to hurt their feelings," "She's my friend; I don't want her to feel bad," and "I don't want to deal with the anger."

One of the sole leaders who indicated he liked to give feedback was sitting in the front row and raised his hand proudly. When he looked around the room, he was stunned to see so few of his fellow leaders raising hands. When asked why he liked to give feedback, his response was, "I like to know where I stand, so I assume others do, too."

Immediately following the initial question, these same 500 leaders were asked how many of them liked to receive feedback, nearly all raised their hands, citing the same reason: "I like to know where I stand."

Digging deeper, when these leaders were asked whether they wanted to hear the bad as well as the good, since it was the negative feedback that they avoided giving, nearly everyone raised their hands. When asked why, the comments universally could be distilled to one: "So that I can improve." When asked whether the employees that reported to them might also want to know the good and the bad, so that they too could improve, the room fell silent.

These utility leaders are not alone.

Most of us want to know where we stand, yet few of us like to give the same feedback to others. Can we then easily conclude that it's not *if* we give feedback, but rather *how* we do it?

The Two-for-One Rule

Think Strategically: What is the Goal of Feedback?

If we think about the purpose or goal of giving feedback, it is both to praise for a job well done and to encourage the person to continue performing her or his best work. Or, it's to help guide the employee to improve. This is the so-called "constructive criticism," which some think is an oxymoron. If, when giving constructive feedback, we "begin with the end in mind" and are strategic, our goal is to have the receiver of the communication hear us out, and to perform differently in future. Getting the other to listen means we want her or him to be receptive, not defensive, and to really hear what we have to say.

A proven method in accomplishing this aim is the "two-for-one" rule, which means two positives for every "aw shucks," or negative. How much kinder and more productive to hear "I am glad you turned the memo in on time and followed the format our department adopted. Thank you. I am confused as to the alternatives pursued. Tell me about the selection process. Did you consider others?" This is a great conversation starter that allows the person giving the feedback to steer the conversation into a constructive remark, such as "I would have also looked into _____ and _____."

Isn't this form of feedback preferable to stating "What were you thinking?" "How could you draw that conclusion?" or "This is all wrong."

Case Study 8.1

After working diligently on a memo at the request of Manny Manager, Suzy Supervisor proudly handed in her proposal to reorganize the office space in her area. She spent hours researching how an open-space configuration might work, checked in with her employees, and even called Desiree Director at a competitor company to learn how she had reorganized her office into an open space.

Manny, however, disliked the concept of an open office space, fearing people would spend too much time chatting and too little time working. Manny neglected to advise Suzy of this, thinking, "Everyone knows that the open space concept leads to lack of productivity." When he read the memo in her presence, he was shaking his head.

His response to her was "No, this is all wrong, how could you think that?" This was heard by Suzy as "you idiot."

What if? Manny had followed the two-for-one rule? Think how Suzy would have accepted the information if Manny had stated, "I guess I forgot to tell you that I have a bias against the open space configuration. Sorry." "I'm glad the memo was turned in early, and I like the research you did. As I stated, I was not expecting this recommendation. In fact, I disagree with it.

"Tell me more and let's see if you can convince me." Suzy quickly picked up on Manny's comment about her research and added, "I didn't include it in the memo. However, there are many studies that show that motivated employees are productive employees and that working in an open space with quick access to team members encourages motivation—hence productivity."

At the end of the conversation, Manny still held firm to his bias, and said "no" to the open office concept. Suzy was unsuccessful in persuading him to her point of view, recognizing on some level that his mind was already made up. There was nothing she could have done to persuade him otherwise. While discouraged, she went back to the drawing board, and developed an alternative plan that was agreeable to Manny.

Timing is Everything

A companion piece to the "two-for-one" rule is "timing is everything." Positive feedback should be given as closely as possible in time to the event, and can also be given in public.

When the feedback is negative, the giver should ensure she or he can be objective and unemotional. It should be given only when the giver has had time to cool down, and it should always be given in private. Delivering the "bad news" should also come as close in time as possible to the event. After all, the goal of constructive or corrective feedback is to improve the receiver's performance.

How does one balance when to give negative feedback? On the one hand, it should be given as close in time as possible to the event to assist the receiver in learning from her or his mistake. On the other hand, to avoid unpleasant or even disastrous results, it should never be given out of anger and always in private.

A good rule of thumb followed by astute leaders is to "praise in public and discipline in private."

Case Study 8.2

Lidia Labor Lawyer worked in a large company. She was a young up-and-comer: ambitious, witty, charming, and a hard worker. One day in February she was called into the office of Eugene Executive, a senior vice president of a large department, to provide guidance on a confidential employee matter.

The executive sought Lidia out, even though her work team had other, more-senior labor lawyers, because in less than a year on the job she had developed a reputation for being smart, fearless, and a strong advocate for her client. In the course of the meeting, Lidia overstepped her boundaries with an uncharacteristically rude comment. She was summarily dismissed from Eugene's office, without being given time to apologize.

As Lidia walked to her office, she feared Bryan Boss would yell at her, but decided that if he didn't say anything about the incident, maybe Eugene wasn't quite as put out as she thought. She decided that she wouldn't say anything either. When she returned, Bryan was his usual affable self, asking Lidia what she was doing for lunch, and inviting her to join him. Lidia thought, "Wow, I skated by this one." The lunch proceeded normally, and Lidia forgot the event.

In late November of the same year, it was time for performance evaluations, to be followed by raises and bonuses. Lidia could hardly wait, for she knew her star was rising. After all, she had been the one in the group to conduct, and subsequently prevail in, the first in-house labor arbitration; the client departments typically asked for her advice and counsel; and, she was considered to be the female who could break the glass ceiling.

In the course of her evaluation, Bryan, who had apparently been contacted by Eugene in February, chewed her out for having been "rude to Eugene Executive." Lidia, never shy, asked why Bryan hadn't told her about it in February, when she could have repaired her relationship with Eugene. Why had he acted as if nothing had happened and then waited until November, when this long-ago event would seemingly impact her raise, bonus and possible promotional opportunities?

Bryan said, "Well, you were—and are—doing such a good job, I didn't want to discourage you." Lidia replied, "But Bryan, I could have apologized to Eugene in February and learned a valuable lesson. Now it seems like this will be held against me. How will this affect my salary increase, bonus and even an opportunity for promotion?" Bryan, somewhat stunned by Lidia's candor, said nothing.

What if? Bryan had followed both the "two-for-one" rule and had been timely in his feedback? The dialogue could have gone along the lines of: "Lidia, I am impressed with how well you have fit into the culture, and how many department heads seek you out for advice. I have to say that knowing you as I do, I was surprised to learn what you said to Eugene Executive yesterday. I'm sure this was a one-off, but if I were you, I'd apologize profusely, and see what you could do to make it up to him."

Feedback that close to the event would have allowed Lidia to own-up to Bryan and to Eugene, apologize to both of them, learn a lesson, and move on. It also would have dispelled any of the negative feelings that Bryan harbored for nearly ten months, and, potentially, allowed her to stay on track in her quest to break the glass ceiling.

Suggestions for Giving Feedback

Follow the two-for-one rule: two positives for every "aw shucks." In addition to being strategic and achieving one's aims (providing feedback that will be received), following the two-for-one rule allows the giver to focus on the positive, which allows him or her to be in a positive space.

Time the Feedback
- Positive feedback should be immediate and can be in public.
- Negative feedback should be when one is cool and unemotional, close in time to the event, and always in private.

The Power of Positive Feedback

Undoubtedly, all of us have communicated dissatisfaction with a product or service we consumed that didn't live up to our expectations. Customer service representatives field these communications day-in and day-out. But how many of us take the time to thank a customer-focused worker, or better yet, to report a positive experience to the individual's supervisor?

Beyond the arena of customer service, how many of us take the time to thank someone who performed a simple act of kindness, or inspired us?

My friend Eleanor shared a poignant story that inspired me to follow her lead. A ballet enthusiast and Canadian, Eleanor attended a performance in her native land shortly before moving to southern California. She was so moved by the performance of one of the dancers that she took the time to handwrite a letter of appreciation and gratitude for the dancer's artistry.

On her initial house scouting journey to southern California, Eleanor and her daughter stayed in a local hotel. The two went to the hotel's dining room and who should Eleanor see but the dancer. Kismet!

Eleanor approached the dancer, apologized for interrupting and introduced herself, mentioning that she was the author of a letter of admiration, asking the dancer whether she had received it. The dancer leaned over, fished in her purse, then sat up straight holding the letter. She was clearly moved by the gift of Eleanor's appreciation and kept that letter with her.

If not moved or inspired by others, all of us have had positive experiences with others we know for brief moments—an in-person customer contact, or a telephone or online customer service person who solved our problem. How many of us take the time, as Eleanor did, to show that appreciation?

How wonderful it would be if we were all to do that. As with practicing the two-for-one rule in the workplace, expressing our appreciation for others that have done something nice for us, or who inspire us, allows us to focus on the positive—which, of course, rebounds back to us.

Remember Simon SVP? After adopting the practice of weekly thanking an employee for something he or she did, or giving an 'attaboy or 'attagirl to someone who "shot the lights out of the park," he not only turned around the perception of his leadership within his own team; he found employees from other departments clamoring to work for him. Further, it had an added impact on Simon: He began focusing on the positive and looking—without being phony or fake—for the best in others.

Tips for Practicing the Two-for-One Rule, Timing is Everything, and the Power of Positive Feedback

- ✓ Focus on what went right while recognizing what went wrong or could have been done better.
- ✓ State the positives first, and then the "aw shucks."
- ✓ Remember to time the feedback—when the giver can be unemotional and state the acts and facts only.
- ✓ Praise in public and discipline in private.
- ✓ Look for opportunities to offer praise.
- ✓ Take the time to express appreciation to those we know, or others we barely or do not know at all, yet still provided us with good service or a kindness, or inspired us to greater heights.

9

PERCEPTION IS REALITY
Assuming Facts Not in Evidence

All of us bring our own individual and collective histories "to the dance." Each of us has enjoyed a unique set of life experiences, from birth through to wherever we are today in our own life's journey. Among many other influences, we are shaped by our families and their histories, the tribe to which we belong, the diverse cultures we experience, our educational involvements, and our work encounters to name a few.

We often hear that our parents are our first teachers. As we grow up, become socialized, and meet other people, we are often surprised to learn that others had different childhood experiences, and thus, react differently than we do to the same set of circumstances. These diverse backgrounds inform what we think and believe, what we assume others think and believe, and act as the basis for our communication.

In the judicial system, the phrase "assuming facts not in evidence" relates to a witness testifying to a "fact" that has yet to be established in the course of a trial. In our daily lives, "assuming facts not in evidence" often means that the communicator assumes that the receiver of the information operates from the same belief system.

In the turbulent times in which we live, "assuming facts not in evidence" can lead to mistrust, anger, and even violence. Still most of us do it on a daily basis. Let's review some of the previous scenarios and case studies where assumption played a negative role.

Revisiting Cecilia CEO

Remember Cecilia CEO from Chapters 1 and 4? She assumed that Edward Executive Assistant knew precisely what she meant when she gave very important instructions (about sending information to selective board members) while walking out the door one evening. That led to disastrous results—the loss of jobs for two employees and untold damage to the corporation.

Revisiting Case Study 6.1

Recall also Penelope PhD, the "I've never taken a 360-degree myself" consultant who gave survey results to Carl Controller, telling him "some people think you are manipulative." Although that information did not lead to devastating or even a hurtful result, since Carl was a fellow 360-degree practitioner and knew enough to challenge her, it surely could have. Most individuals hearing that others in their peer group believe them to be manipulative would have been crushed.

That situation is instructive from multiple perspectives. Think about the person or persons who made the statement that Carl was manipulative. They had assumed that anyone, in this case a fellow board member, who would recommend a candidate for employment would only do so to control the function within the company.

Think again about Penelope PhD, who told Carl Controller that his peers found him manipulative. Presumably she assumed that he would find the feedback helpful—why else would she have imparted that information? If the goal of this type of feedback—"constructive criticism"—is to help a recipient change behavior, would advising someone that others said he or she was manipulative be constructive? Penelope PhD missed the mark.

Think about Carl, the receiver of this information, being told that others believe he is manipulative. This would likely have the effect of being hurtful or confusing, and perhaps make him want to lash out. What is the likelihood that the information given in this format would have been helpful?

Revisiting Case Study 3.2

Remember Felicity and Jasmine, the two volunteers assigned to work the major fundraiser for the national volunteer association? Each assumed the other would communicate in the style each preferred. This couldn't have been further from the truth.

Felicity, who was of the "tell me once, and if you repeat it, I'll think you assume I'm an idiot" mindset, gave Jasmine information once, and assumed she would get it. At the same, Jasmine, who preferred the "say it once, and then please follow it up with an e-mail" style continued to follow-up all verbal communications with an e-mail. This led to confusion, anger, and hostility between the two.

All of this could easily have been avoided had the two spent a few minutes deciding how best to communicate with one another as opposed to assuming each shared the same style as the other.

Revisiting Case Study 7.1

And then there was Jacob, the director for the large product development firm who worked with Calvin CEO to develop a plan to roll out a new compensation system. Although Calvin was engaged at the outset of the project, once it was set in motion, he assumed Jacob would take the ball and run. Calvin perceived that a plan was in place and Jacob would simply execute.

If Calvin stayed involved appropriately in an oversight capacity, he would have learned that Jacob didn't know who to contact to benchmark his compensation thinking and was behind schedule. Had Calvin learned this, he could have made adjustments. Calvin could have added more resources to the project, delayed the final implementation date, or shortened or even eliminated some of the steps.

Calvin's error was in assuming that once the work plan was set in place, it would become reality.

Case Study 9.1

Anita Accountant worked for an audit firm. She had recently married and mentioned to her office mates that she hoped to start a family. Nothing more was said. About six months later, Anita's office was hired to conduct a multi-month audit in a neighboring state. The position, which was a promotion for Anita, would set her on a path to become a partner, which was her goal.

During the interview process for the promotion, Stanley Senior Partner asked her when she planned to start a family. Anita was shocked, and blurted out, "You can't ask me that; it's against the law. It shouldn't have any bearing on whether or not I get the job. As a matter of fact, my husband plans to stay home when we have a child."

Anita was not promoted; Miquel Male Colleague was. Anita filed a complaint of discrimination with the Equal Employment Opportunity Commission. It was now time for Stanley Senior Partner to be shocked. Clearly, Miquel was more qualified than Anita—he had more years of experience, specifically with the industry in question.

What went Wrong? Based upon office gossip, Stanley perceived and concluded that Anita planned to start a family, and he also assumed that when she did, having a child would prevent her from taking the assignment out of state. The question he asked to support his perception and assumption was unlawful. However, Stanley's concern was legitimate—that if Anita couldn't perform some of the tasks and duties of the new position, then she wasn't the right candidate. How could Stanley have learned the information he needed to assist in making the job decision without running afoul of the law?

Had Stanley posed the question this way: "This position requires a considerable amount of out-of-state travel. Specifically, for the next six to nine months, the person in this position will be required to spend

80% of the time out of state. Is there anything that would prevent you from doing this?"

This request is neutral, fact-based, and displays no preconceived perceptions or assumptions. Frankly, it should be asked of all candidates. Who knows, maybe Miquel has a child care commitment, or perhaps he's taking a class to further his education, caring for an elderly parent, or doesn't want to spend that kind of time away from home.

Tips for Overcoming Perceptions and Assumptions

✓ Engage in self-reflection—determine which perceptions or assumptions you might have and challenge yourself not to give in to them.

✓ Follow the adage of "walking a mile in another's shoes, moccasins, high heels, jack boots, or flip flops." How might someone else perceive or respond to the situation at hand?

✓ When in doubt, ask neutrally phrased questions.

10

THE STING OF EMOTIONAL COMMUNICATION
Using Neutral Language in the Workplace

We humans are a bundle of many things. We are intellectual, rational, and emotional beings. A good rule to follow in the workplace is that "it's okay to have emotions, since we all do, and it's okay to describe those emotions. However, it's not okay to display those emotions or to act them out."

There are many good reasons for this. It helps to avoid saying something that is later regretted. (If we do give in and say a regrettable thing, apologize, since we all make mistakes.) It also avoids hurting others and allows for thinking and rethinking an initial tendency to use fighting words. It allows for the rational part of who we are to overtake the emotional part. Words can be swords or shields, and the words we chose can unite or divide us.

One has to look no further than the public discourse on many social and cultural issues, often based upon an individual's personal religious or spiritual beliefs. There is also our current political climate, where those who hold different beliefs are considered enemies, stupid, or even traitors.

The language heard today in the public square is often used as a sword to divide us, by appealing to base fear, loathing, and hatred, rather than to unite us. Sadly, when acted upon, these fighting words can, and have, resulted in violence.

Consider the topic of pregnancy termination, and the language used to describe it. Those who believe that it is a woman's right to choose whether to terminate a pregnancy, will characterize themselves as "pro-choice," and view those who oppose this position as "anti-choice."

Those who believe that pregnancy termination is inherently wrong refer to themselves as "pro-life," and those who believe the opposite are "pro-abortion."

Termination late in a pregnancy is referred to by pro-choice individuals as "late-term abortion," while those in opposition consider it "partial-birth abortion." The descriptions are graphic and could be called fighting words. Can't one be pro-life (for herself) and pro-choice (for others)?

Emotionally-laden language in the workplace tends to focus on work assignments and performance. "You're not pulling your weight," "What were you thinking?" "How could anyone think this would work?" or "That's the dumbest idea I've ever heard," to repeat a few.

Not only do these statements work counter to the intended effect, which is to get the best out of someone else, they also serve to delegitimize the person making those statements, and therefore allow the receiver to discount the information. "There goes old Joe again, just ignore him, he'll get over it." Or, "What an idiot, why would I listen to her?"

Case Study 10.1

Beatrice Benefits Administrator went into Hillary HR VP's office to complain about a work assignment. "Why should I have to do this? It's not in my area of responsibility, and besides I don't have the time." Hillary repeated that when she gave the assignment to Beatrice, she would also reassign some of Beatrice's current work to enable her to do the job. Hillary reminded Beatrice that she had been selected to complete the project because of her technical expertise.

Beatrice again stated that she didn't want to do the assignment, and besides had too much other work. Hillary responded neutrally and in the same manner as before.

The third time Beatrice leveled her complaint at Hillary, she added, "Besides you don't like me, so you're setting me up for failure."

At this point, having stated the acts and facts several times, Hillary was starting to get angry. Afraid that she might act out those emotions by saying something that both of them would regret, Hillary declared, "Beatrice, you need to leave my office now."

Beatrice stayed seated, refusing to leave Hillary's office, so Hillary walked out and went into a conference room.

That night, Hillary thought long and hard about what had happened, about her role in the transaction and whether she would have changed anything. The fact was, Hillary didn't like Beatrice. Hillary contemplated whether to assign the project to someone else, and what to do next. She called her outside advisor, explained the situation, and asked for advice. Her advisor agreed with Hillary's handling of the matter and that Beatrice should be tasked with the assignment.

Both agreed that Hillary should discuss the matter with Beatrice the following day. She should specifically reiterate the job expectations and address Beatrice's seeming refusal to do the job. Beatrice would be insubordinate if she failed or refused to complete the assignment.

The next day, Hillary called Beatrice into her office and stated, "Beatrice, I asked you to leave my office last night because I was angry. I am still angry now, and let me tell you why." Hillary then reiterated the nature and scope of the assignment, her willingness to reassign other work that was on Beatrice's plate, and that Beatrice's failure or refusal to complete the assignment would be insubordination for which she would be disciplined up to and including termination of employment.

Beatrice sat quietly, unable to dismiss Hillary's cool, calm description of her anger or to minimize or trivialize the importance and impact of the content of the meeting. In the end, Beatrice did the project to Hillary's satisfaction.

What Worked

Hillary HR VP explained the acts and facts of her decision to assign the project to Beatrice. After repeating herself in a calm and neutral manner several times, Hillary recognized that she was beginning to anger, and as a result might say something that would have been fueled by emotion, not logic or the facts.

Accordingly, Hillary adjourned the meeting, allowing her to think about what happened, to seek advice, to be strategic, and consider the goal. In the end, she, along with advice from her outside advisor, confirmed that the assignment was appropriately made, and that the choice was now Beatrice's—either she could complete the assignment or if she failed or refused to do so, be found insubordinate and face disciplinary action.

Hillary described being angry in a calm manner, rather than acting it out. This proved to have had the intended effect on Beatrice, who was not able to dismiss or trivialize Hillary's leadership. In the end, the goal was achieved, and Beatrice completed the job to Hillary's satisfaction.

What if? Hillary had given into her anger? Think what could have gone wrong. After patiently repeating herself three times, and asking Beatrice to leave her office, Hillary blurted out in a loud voice, "Listen, Beatrice, I've had about as much as I can take putting up with your attitude. I'm not discussing this any longer—do the assignment or else." Beatrice would have felt vindicated, saying, "See, I'm right, you just gave me this assignment because you don't like me." Worse yet, she would have dismissed Hillary and Hillary's authority over her.

Tips to Avoid the Sting of Emotional Communication

✓ Avoid communicating when angry. You can always come back another day and describe your anger without giving into it, which can be very powerful.

✓ Select words and language that are neutral.

✓ Be strategic: Remember what the goal is and drive to achieve it.

✓ Seek outside advice when unsure.

11

WORKPLACE COMMUNICATION IN THE ERA OF TECHNOLOGY

The Internet has spawned a multiplicity of ways in which to communicate, or miscommunicate as the case may be. Twitter, blogs, Facebook, Instagram, texts, and e-mail are among them. In the workplace, e-mail and texts are the predominant technological tools of communication, and this chapter will focus on those two.

Prior to the Internet, written communication in the workplace largely came in the form of memos, ranging from post-it note size to several full-sized pages. The admonition about written communication then continues to be a good rule of thumb today: "Don't write anything you wouldn't want your mother to read on the front page of the *LA Times, New York Times,* etc."

The speed of Internet communication results in many of us acting like the trumpet (thought, to fingers, to launch), when acting like the French horn (thinking first, then writing, and launching) would likely serve us better. How many times have we acted first and thought second? How many e-mails or texts have we written and sent, almost simultaneously wishing we could retract?

And then there is the longevity of Internet communication: Think of it as lasting forever and being visible to many more than those to whom it was intended. Just ask Oliver North about the e-mails that came back to haunt him in the Iran-Contra affair.

Tips that Apply to E-mail and Texts

✓ Be strategic. "Begin with the end in mind." What is the goal to be accomplished with the communication?

✓ Some things are better handled in person or with a phone call, particularly sensitive matters.

✓ Does it meet the "front page of the *LA Times*" test?

✓ Is it being sent and copied to the appropriate people? The carbon-copy (Cc:) function on e-mails is viewed by some as the "snitch" factor. Did the person's colleagues, boss, or others really need to have the information?

✓ Write it first, save it as a draft, and then reread it later to ensure that it says what you intended—especially if you are acting on impulse, while emotional, or specifically, when angry.

✓ Ask another to read it and give feedback about what she or he believes is being communicated.

✓ Check to ensure the language and tone are neutral.

Tips Unique to E-mail

✓ E-mails last forever on back-up servers, even when deleted. Carefully consider whether the communication is one that would meet the test of time.

✓ Use the subject line strategically and tactically.

✓ If a meeting notice, state: Communications Team Meeting, January 5th at 2:00 p.m. in the Board Room.

✓ If timing is critical, state who or what the meeting is for, and the date, time, and location of the meeting: "Response needed by end of day," or, "Response needed within 24 hours."

✓ If timing is not important or not critical, state: "Action Requested by _____."

✓ If copying a group where no action is sought state: "For information only."

✓ Send the e-mail to the person or persons who need to act. Use the Cc: only for those who may need to know—and remember the perception of the "snitch" factor.

✓ Use the response feature most e-mail systems have. Get an alert when the e-mail has been opened.

✓ If timing is critical and the person has not yet responded, a second gentle reminder in the subject line could follow "Friendly Reminder, Need Your Input by End of Day."

✓ If all else fails, pick up the phone, or walk around the corner and talk to the person.

Tips Unique to Text Messages

✓ Find out if the recipient accepts text messages.

✓ Send to more than one person if she or he really needs to know about the content of the text.

✓ Read the content before sending: autocorrect can make for unintelligible—and sometimes extremely inappropriate—messages.

✓ Acronyms have run amok: make sure the receiver knows what they mean be it BTW, LOL, IMO, or the like.

✓ Avoid emojis.

Case Study 11.1

Carol Colleague worked in a small, tight-knit nonprofit. She loved all kinds of jewelry and wore several pieces to work each day. She didn't discriminate among costume jewelry, plastic pieces, manufactured gemstones, or the real things. She purchased most of her jewelry, and some were family heirlooms to which she attached sentimental value. Carol wore them all.

Frequently, she would take off pieces while working and over time lost some. Carol thought she had seen a piece or two worn by others and let it slide. One day Carol believed that a family heirloom she had lost was on the arm of a colleague. Frustrated and angry, she went into her office and sent the following e-mail to her entire office.

Subject Line: Who Stole my Mother's Bracelet?

To the staff:

You all know that I love jewelry because you often compliment me on what I'm wearing. I used to think that I was careless and lost some of my pieces. I now know that's not true because I've seen some of you wearing them. I'm sick and tired of this. Today, my Mother's green jade bracelet was on one of your arms. I would like that person to bring it back to me and apologize.

Sincerely,

Carol Colleague

The Response

It's not hard to imagine that all of Carol's colleagues were offended, felt accused, and were angry. A few brave souls sought Carol out to tell her how hurt and offended they were, that they would never steal from her or anyone else, and demanded an apology.

Others who were either fearful of Carol's anger, or were too intimidated by her e-mail to respond, reported their feelings to the HR Manager and the non-profit's CEO. One, a quiet and valued member of the team, considered resigning because she was so upset.

What Went Wrong?

Starting at the beginning, was this an appropriate topic for e-mail, or would this information have been better handled by a discrete conversation between Carol and the individual Carol believed was wearing her mother's jade bracelet? Did she "assume facts not in evidence"?

If Carol decided to communicate via e-mail, should it have been sent to the entire office? Was the subject line appropriate?

Did Carol act out of impulse and/or anger? Were the words chosen and the tone used designed to achieve her goal (which, presumably was to find her mother's jade bracelet and to get it back)? Did she accept responsibility for any of what transpired via "I" statements?

What If: Carol went into her office, took the famous 15-second pause, "cooled her jets," and decided that in the afternoon she would see if she could have what likely would be an awkward conversation with her colleague. It went along the following lines:

"Sarah, do you have a few minutes to discuss a personal matter with me? You do, great. I bet you've noticed that I like to wear jewelry to work. I sometimes can be careless with it, taking off rings and bracelets, especially when I use the computer or the copier.

Recently, I was wearing one of my favorite pieces—a jade bracelet that belonged to my mother, and silly me, I must have taken it off somewhere and can't find it. This morning, I noticed you were wearing a jade bracelet, and was hoping beyond hope that I left it somewhere and perhaps you found it and would pop on over to my office.

That said, now that I'm in your office, I can see that you are wearing a jade bracelet, but different from the one I lost. I'm going to send an e-mail to the office to be on the look-out for it, and hope you will too. Thanks for your time."

What If? Carol had then returned to her office and sent out the following e-mail:

Subject Line: HELP—I Lost my Mother's Jade Bracelet: Has Anyone Seen it?

Dear Team:

I did something foolish the other day—I took off one of my pieces of jewelry (my mother's jade bracelet to be exact) while working, and can't find it. I have loads of bracelets, and this one is very special to me. I would be beyond grateful if all of you would keep a lookout for it.

Thanks so much,

Carol Colleague

Case Study 11.2

Catalina Consultant served as an interim manager for a prestigious membership club that counted the city's well-regarded professionals and company executives as members of its Board of Directors. One such professional—a doctor—sent her a dirty joke on the club's e-mail system. Catalina was shocked that he would do such a thing. She didn't want to offend the board member, yet she knew enough to know that the e-mail and her response, or nonresponse, would live on the server forever, and that a new club manager might well find it. Catalina knew she needed to act.

After taking the 15-second pause, Catalina responded to the offending board member, and copied the Board President.

Subject Line: My Private E-mail is _____

Dear Dr. Jones:

I am enjoying my tenure as the interim club manager and getting to know and work with the board. Please know that the club's e-mail address is for business matters only. Any other information should be directed to my private e-mail address, which is _____.

Thank you for your attention to this matter.

Very truly yours,

Catalina, Interim Club Manager

The e-mail did the trick. Not only did the Board President, a colleague of Dr. Jones, chide him about sending "off-color" stories and suggest that he not do so, Catalina immediately blocked Dr. Jones when he sent another dirty joke to her personal e-mail.

A few months later, a permanent manager was hired, Catalina went on to another consulting job and periodically ran into Dr. Jones. The two had civil and restrained conversations with one another.

Several years later, the manager ran into Catalina and mentioned that he had recently been searching the club's online files for a document, and found the e-mail exchange between Catalina and Dr. Jones, noting that Catalina had included the then board president on her e-mail response. Catalina advised the club manager that she had subsequently blocked Dr. Jones. Catalina was never so glad that she took the actions she did.

Tips to Effective Communication in the Era of Technology

✓ Slow down and think—does it pass the front page of the *LA Times* test?

✓ Avoid acronyms and emojis.

✓ Use the subject line of emails strategically—why should the receiver read it?

✓ Consider whether a face-to-face or phone call would be more effective.

THE POWERS OF APOLOGY AND HUMILITY IN THE WORKPLACE

When any group is asked, "Who has made a mistake in this room?" all raise their hands. When next asked, "How many have apologized for these mistakes?" fewer keep their hands in the air. Thus, the question isn't if we make mistakes; the important question is how do we handle them?

Some believe that admitting to mistakes is a sign of weakness, while others believe it is a show of strength. It takes little courage to make a mistake. It takes real courage to admit one has made a mistake and to apologize for having done so.

Wouldn't you rather hear "I'm sorry, I made a mistake and I apologize," "I was wrong, sorry about that," "I goofed, and I apologize," or "Guess I was confused, now I understand," rather than hearing a long excuse as to why the mistake was made?

An excuse typically involves an attempt to absolve the person who made the mistake, and often places blame on someone or something else, usually the receiver of the communication. "You didn't understand me," "You misinterpreted what I said," or "If you (or Jane or Joe) had given me the correct information, I wouldn't have done it that way."

Any way one looks at it, it's an excuse rather than an apology. "Oops, I didn't see that, wish I had. I goofed," and "Sorry about that" sounds—and feels—so much better.

The courage to apologize goes hand-in-hand with using "I" statements rather than "you" statements. It requires the person to own up—to accept responsibility for his or her misunderstanding, confusion, misstatements, or mistakes.

Illustration in Real Time

A recent media story depicted a male blogger commenting on the attire of a newly elected Congresswoman. When the comment was met with universal condemnation—from those of all political persuasions, rather than apologizing he commented along the lines of "I didn't mean that. People misconstrued what I said."

How much better it would have been had the blogger said, "I'm sorry, that was insensitive of me."

Equal Treatment

To be fair, men commenting negatively on a woman's attire violates a cardinal rule of communication between the sexes. On the other hand, a woman dissolving into tears also violates a cardinal rule of communication between the sexes in the workplace.

Case Study 12.1

Maria, the newly-hired Communications Director in a homeless shelter agreed in the job interview process that, if selected for the position, she would talk to several homeless individuals and write articles to feature in fundraising appeals. This task was emphasized in the interview. She was also advised that the Communications Department was essentially a two-person shop.

While settling into her position, Maria asked a colleague, Dwayne in the Development Department, if he wouldn't mind helping out by conducting the interviews. Dwayne was happy to help Maria during her introductory period. Six months later Dwayne was still conducting the interviews and Maria simply "forgot" to assume this responsibility. Dwayne asked Maria about it, and she said "I'm understaffed, and can't do it. You have a larger staff, why don't you just take this on indefinitely?"

Dwayne went to his boss, Darla Development Department VP, who, in turn, went to the Chief Operating Officer, the person to whom both Darla and

Maria reported. The COO, who participated in the interview process and knew that Maria was to have been responsible for interviewing homeless individuals, called all of the parties into his office to discuss the matter.

During the course of the meeting the COO reminded Maria that she agreed that if selected she would take on this assignment. He also reminded Maria that he described to her that the Communications groups was relatively small, with limited resources.

Maria expressed frustration about the low level of staffing in her department and started to cry, accusing her colleagues of treating her unfairly. The COO immediately backed down, advising Dwayne that interviewing homeless was now his assignment.

After the meeting both Dwayne and Darla were upset, believing that the COO backed down because of Maria's tears and unsubstantiated allegations of unfair treatment. Neither Dwayne nor his boss ever asked the COO for clarification or discussed the matter with him further. However, both Dwayne and Darla believed the COO "caved" because Maria cried.

The relationships were never repaired.

What Went Wrong?

What if the COO had stated when Maria started crying, "Maria, I'm sorry if this is uncomfortable. Should we adjourn the meeting and reconvene later?" Or what if the COO handed Maria a box of tissues and asked whether she wanted to continue the meeting or reconvene later?

Then, at a reconvened meeting, the COO could have stated the acts and facts and said, "Maria, please remember that during the job interview, we described that an important part of this job would entail interviewing homeless individuals. We also said that the Communications group was small.

"We are a team-based environment and Dwayne was happy to assist with this assignment while you were acclimating to the job and the environment. Unfortunately, he has many of his own assignments and can no longer assist. We need you to take this task on.

"In addition, Maria, I was surprised to learn about possible unfair treatment. Please report to human resources so that an investigation into the matter can begin."

Humility at Work

All accomplishments and praise go to the team, while all mistakes are owned by the leader. That's what inspirational leaders do. As President Harry Truman said, "The buck stops here." The opportunity for leaders to be humble presents itself frequently, if not daily, and there are real benefits that follow.

The leader that takes credit for the work of her or his subordinates breeds distrust and, at times, contempt from the team. The leader who acknowledges the work of subordinates and takes responsibility for mistakes, whether his or her own or members of the team, breeds loyalty and trust.

Another important act of workplace humility is to know one's strengths and weaknesses, and to recognize both with honesty and candor. Often that means assembling a team with complementary strengths to achieve the goal.

Remember the HR team from Chapter 2? The group put together a winning project to expand the workers in a building and construction firm by one-third. The team accomplished the goal by putting together all of the needed department representatives—with the applicable skills and resources—to get the job done.

Other times humility means knowing when to bow out of a promotion or an offered assignment that would be a stretch too far.

Case Study 12.2

Marla Manager, an engineer, was a young up-and-comer in a multinational oil company. Because she was on the fast-track to the C-Suite, the senior leadership offered her several cross-training assignments, promotions, and opportunities to prove her stripes. Her record was stellar.

One of the positions, a coveted promotion to the lobbying group within the company, appeared to be a stretch too far for Marla. Six months into the job, during which Marla had written great documents but stumbled during oral presentations, she concluded she was doing her Company—and herself—no good. Marla went to her mentor and asked to be returned to her former position.

Marla's wish was granted—she was indeed demoted, with salary taken away. In the end, she rose to become Chief Financial Officer of this Company. Her humility, honesty, candor—and great courage—paid off.

The Turbulent Times in Which We Live

Sadly, in the sum total world of "I win, you lose," the lessons of personal responsibility and humility appear to be fading away. However, there are examples to draw upon.

In the book *Notorious RBG,* the authors quote one of Supreme Court Justice Ruth Bader Ginsburg's law clerks about how to address those who lose. The Justice instructs that the "important takeaway for them is not just 'I lost.' It should be 'I was treated fairly and understand the judiciary.'"

The book contrasts that style with Justice Antonin Scalia who was quoted as saying, "I think when it's wrong, it should be destroyed."

Consider which of the two justices was more effective at explaining the Court's position—particularly to the side that lost?

As with the overtly emotional boss at work, Justice Scalia's less-than-humble remarks could be easily dismissed as, "Oh, that's just Scalia. Don't let it bother you, that's just the way he is. No one else pays attention, why should you."

One is far more open to learning from the humbler approach of Justice Bader Ginsburg. And, isn't that the point?

Remember Beatrice Benefits Administrator from Chapter 10? She remained in Hillary HR VP's office long after Hillary had confirmed the assignment of a work project to her. Beatrice continued to state her objections, and Hillary ultimately asked her to leave her office. When Beatrice failed to do so, Hillary left.

The following morning Hillary called Beatrice into her office stating, "Beatrice, I asked you to leave my office last night because I was angry. I am still angry now and let me tell you why."

Imagine if Hillary had acted on her anger the previous evening, raising her voice, and saying something she might regret? Beatrice could have easily dismissed Hillary with a, "Oh, there she goes again."

Another Example of the Powers of Apology and Humility

President George H.W. Bush was famous for his humble approach to leadership, which at times was viewed as weak or wimpish. He was, perhaps, the ultimate behind-the-scenes leader, sending hand-written notes of gratitude to others, and bearing his presidential loss with dignity and grace. It has been reported that the President to whom he lost—Bill Clinton—became his "adopted son."

When interviewed by his newscaster granddaughter (Jenna Bush Hager) on June 12th, 2012 (his 89th birthday), he was asked what he wanted to be remembered for. He stated "I want somebody else to define the legacy, I'm kinda bad at the use of the 'L' word. *People will point out what I did wrong, and what we did right.*"

Tips for Executing the Powers of Apology and Humility

✓ Accept responsibility for your actions: own up and apologize.
✓ Never blame others for misunderstandings, confusion, or perceptions. Be the master of your ship: clarify and apologize.
✓ Give credit to the team, and accept blame for the mistakes.
✓ Recognize your strengths and weaknesses and act on them accordingly.

(13)

THAT'S A WRAP

We communicate all of the time in many different ways: verbally, in writing, through the Internet, by the way we stand, sit and walk, by what we wear, and how we chose to project ourselves in the world. In so doing, we create perceptions about ourselves in others. We are the only ones that can impact and change those perceptions, if we want to.

In today's turbulent world where words are increasingly used as swords, sparking confusion, hurt feelings, and even violence, it is all the more important that we think first, and communicate second. Our words have consequences, and we are the only ones who can control what and how we communicate.

This practical guide to leadership has highlighted some of the important aspects of communication in the workplace. The easy-to-implement tips found in each chapter require affirmative action on behalf of the communicator. Some of the tips are simpler to incorporate into our workplace tool kits than others. Some require self-reflection and taking the time to think before acting.

All of the tips are tried-and-true and have benefitted thousands who have implemented some or all of them. A quick summary of the tips follows.

Chapter 1

Tips to Ensuring You are Understood: Getting Another to Do What you Want

✓ Communicate to people in the manner they best take in information.
✓ Let her or him know what is to be achieved and the important role he or she will play.

✓ Repeat the desired result in the same or a different communication method: "If you don't get them on the swings, get them on the merry-go-round...."
✓ Check for understanding.
✓ Show appreciation for a task well done.
✓ Show flexibility and a willingness to roll up one's sleeves and help.

Chapter 2

Tips for Making it Easy for Them to Say Yes

✓ Recognize that the decision makers are busy people with multiple projects in front of them.
✓ To ensure success, anticipate and plan for all of the steps needed to complete the project.
✓ Be clear, concise, and thorough. And as it is oft said, "Be brief, be brilliant, be gone."
✓ Assume responsibility for execution.
✓ Do it!

Chapter 3

Tips for Practicing the Platinum Rule: Getting the Best Out of Others

✓ Determine how best the recipient will understand the communication. Ask how the recipient likes to receive information, observe, and/ or try different methods and modes.

✓ Check for understanding.
✓ Flex one's style to meet the others' needs.

Chapter 4

Tips for Strategic Communication

✓ "Begin with the end in mind." What is the goal to be achieved with the communication?
✓ Develop tactics to support the strategy. What needs to be done to achieve the strategic objective?
✓ Work backwards from the goal.
✓ Ensure that all others involved are informed and understand what their respective roles are.

Chapter 5

Tips for Listening, Asking, and Telling

✓ Listen and ask more, tell less.
✓ Announce your intentions by reflecting upon—and sharing—why you are asking.
✓ Adopt Mel's ground rules: When you seek input from others, determine whether you are almost there. Do you simply need confirmation? Do you need all good ideas? What will you do with them—will you implement them?
✓ If those you asked developed a solution that will work, do not substitute your "very good solution" for theirs (remember the Corporate Secretary).

Chapter 6

Tips for Using "I" Statements and Using Acts and Facts

✓ Assume responsibility for the communication. "I believe this," "I heard this," "I don't understand why this happened," "I observed," "I noticed," to state a few.

✓ Think and speak for the one person over which the communicator has control—yourself.

✓ State what happened or didn't happen neutrally. "I asked for the report to be turned in today by noon. I haven't seen it yet," "Some board colleagues think that you recommended a new finance manager so you could run the finance department," or "I noticed that the meeting was cancelled, please tell me why."

✓ Avoid drawing conclusions, stating opinions, or attributing motives to others.

Chapter 7

Tips for Checking for Understanding

✓ Ask "I want to make sure I was clear. Please repeat what you understood me to say."

✓ Request confirmation. "Great conversation. Please go back to your office and e-mail me with how you plan to proceed."

✓ Manage by walking around. Check in to ensure the task, duty or project is on target.

✓ Off-load other work, when possible.

✓ Help, when needed.

Chapter 8

Tips for Practicing the Two-for-One Rule, Timing is Everything, and The Power of Positive Feedback

✓ Focus on what went right while recognizing what went wrong or could have been done better.

✓ State the positives first, and then the "aw shucks."

✓ Remember to time the feedback—when the giver can be unemotional and state the acts and facts only.

✓ Praise in public and discipline in private.

✓ Look for opportunities to offer praise.

✓ Take the time to express appreciation to those we know, others we barely or do not know at all, yet still provided us with good service or a kindness, or inspired us to greater heights.

Chapter 9

Tips for Overcoming Perceptions and Assumptions

✓ Engage in self-reflection—determine what perceptions or assumptions you might have and challenge yourself not to give in to them.

✓ Follow the adage of "walking a mile in another's shoes, moccasins, high heels, jack boots, or flip flops." How might someone else perceive or respond to the situation at hand?

✓ When in doubt, ask neutrally phrased questions.

Chapter 10

Tips to Avoid the Sting of Emotional Communication

✓ Avoid communicating when angry. You can always come back another day and describe your anger without giving into it. Very powerful.
✓ Select words and language that are neutral.
✓ Be strategic: Remember what the goal is and drive to achieve it.
✓ Seek outside advice when unsure.

Chapter 11

Tips to Effective Communication in the Era of Technology

✓ Slow down and think—does it pass the front page of the *LA Times* test?
✓ Avoid acronyms and emojis.
✓ Use the subject line of emails strategically—why should the receiver read it?
✓ Consider whether a face-to-face or phone call would be more effective.

Chapter 12

Tips for Executing the Powers of Apology and Humility

✓ Accept responsibility for your actions: own up and apologize.
✓ Never blame others for misunderstandings, confusion, or perceptions. Be the master of your ship: clarify and apologize.
✓ Give credit to the team, and accept blame for the mistakes.
✓ Recognize your strengths and weaknesses and act on them accordingly.

Closing Thoughts

Control the hell out of the things over which you have control, and forget the rest. Since the one and only thing you have control over is yourself, control what you think about others, what you say to others, how you write (blog, email, text or tweet) about others, how you treat others, and how you want others to perceive you.

If we all did this, followed our higher angels, and rejected our "lizard brains," what a wonderful world it would be.

—Namaste

Made in the USA
San Bernardino, CA
21 February 2019